# His Plan,
# Many Blessings

# His Plan, Many Blessings

## Heather Kruep, MA

# His Plan, Many Blessings

## Heather Kruep, MA

Cover by Isabel Guardian

Scriptures marked NIV taken from *Mom's Devotional Bible, New International Version.* Copyright ©1996 by the Zondervan Corporation. Grand Rapids, Michigan.

Scriptures marked NLT taken from *Everyday Matters Bible for Women, New Living Translation.* Copyright © 2012 by Hendrickson Publishers Marketing, LLC.

**Disclaimer:** This publication is sold with the understanding that the author is not a psychological or medical professional, nor an expert in theology. Please consult with a pastor, medical or psychological professional, if needed. Some details of the content in this book have been omitted to protect the privacy of all involved. Please note apart from the writer's immediate family, the names in this book have been changed to protect identities.

**Website:** www.planfaith.com

ISBN: 978-1-387-79526-0

Printed in the United States of America

Dear God, I made a promise to you to write this book.
It may have taken nearly three years, but it's complete thanks
to your encouragement and guidance.
May your will be done.
Amen.

# His Plan, Many Blessings
# Table of Contents

# His Plan, Many Blessings
# Table of Contents

# Preface

"How do you do it? You must be supermom!"

This is often what I hear when I say I am a homeschooling mother of six children and work full time. I always pause a bit when I hear this question because I know I don't deserve the credit for what I do. God does, but I am often too shy to say it.

I have a great deal of support, but my biggest source of help comes from the Holy Spirit. I have no other explanation for how I can not only function with chronic sleep deprivation but do each task with joy and passion.

My goal in writing this book is to share how I have come to know Jesus, and why I follow Him. I briefly discuss each era to show God's plan for my life unfold.

I want to assure you that no matter how hopeless your own situation seems or how deep into sin you are, God can turn it all around and give you a life that is more enjoyable and fulfilling than you ever imagined.

I also hope to provide comfort and guidance to those who have taken the road less traveled and followed God's nudge to homeschool and/or have a larger family. I will give you a glimpse of how my household runs as a large, homeschooling family.

Lastly, I will provide tips on how to follow God's plan for your life. Most importantly, the encouragement and insights are backed up by scripture.

*May the God of hope fill you with all joy and peace as you trust in him, so that you may overflow with hope by the power of the Holy Spirit.*
*- Romans 15:13 NIV*

# Part 1: Growing Up

# Childhood

*For you created my inmost being; you knit me together in my mother's womb. I praise you because I am fearfully and wonderfully made; your works are wonderful, I know that full well.*
*-Psalm 139:13-14 NIV*

God is with us even before we are born! There were times I felt His presence when I was a child but did not realize it at the time. I prayed often, mainly about the safety of my family. I was an anxious child and worried a lot. Sometimes, I would forget what I was worrying about and would re-trace my thoughts to figure it out. There were times I'd be lying in bed worrying, and suddenly I'd get tired and let sleep take over. I believe that was God's peace coming upon me. God was helping me even before I truly knew Him.

Growing up, my family and I went to church on a regular basis. Church was like a second home. We were involved with choir, bells, and youth group. We participated in Christmas plays and went to summer bible school. The group of kids who also attended our church were like siblings. On Sunday mornings, we would sing children's bible songs together before church. We went on field trips and had holiday parties together too.

While I went to church on a regular basis, I never fully understood the gospel. I believed in God, but I did not pay attention enough to really learn about repentance or Jesus' life, death, and resurrection. I was not taught that the devil does, in fact, exist and works to keep people from God. I don't remember the devil ever being mentioned in the church I attended while growing up. I'm sure they did talk about it, but I just wasn't paying attention. I was clueless, and that made me the perfect target.

*Stay alert! Watch out for your great enemy, the devil. He prowls around like a roaring lion, looking for someone to devour.*
*- 1 Peter 5:8 NLT*

I grew up in the 1980s and 1990s, a time much different from the age of technology and social media. The neighborhood kids and I would be outside every chance we had. Relationships seemed closer then, likely because interactions were more frequent and in person. We played on swing sets, built forts, climbed trees, hiked and played on dirt piles as new houses were being constructed. There were sleepovers in basements, club houses and tents in the backyard. Like the kids I went to church with, neighbors were like family. During the winter months, we would go outside after dinner and play in the snow until we could not stand the cold any longer. Parents were not as hands-on back then. They did not feel the need to watch our every move. Kids were allowed to roam around the subdivision without the neighbors accusing lack of supervision and without the fear of abductions. Kids playing outside without adult supervision was the norm.

When I wasn't outside playing, I was usually out and about with my family. Nearly every Friday night, my family and I would go to the mall. We often ate at Chic-fil-A which at the time was a tiny place tucked in between stores in the mall. After we ate dinner, my dad would sit and watch my brother and me run around the center foyer while my mom went shopping. The foyer had a pit with benches and trees with a lot of space for kids to run around and make friends. I may have been a worrier, but I was a happy child. I found joy in everything. When I learned the word "optimistic," I declared that it was my way of thinking. I always looked on the bright side of things, a character trait that I got from my dad.

Shopping can be boring for kids, but I always chose a favorite feature for every store we went to. Best Buy had keyboards I liked to play on. Menards had an upstairs and a lot of neat things to look at. Kids R Us had games to play. Grocery stores often had samples of new food to try. No matter where we went, I was happy just to be with my family.

# Dog Attack

*God is our refuge and strength, always ready to help in times of trouble.*
*-Psalm 46:1 NLT*

Most of my childhood was safe and uneventful. But one day, my life flashed before my eyes. I was in the 5th grade. I went out to ride my bike. I was filled with dread when I got to the top of the hill and saw two German Shepherds. These dogs were known as a subdivision nuisance. I did not want them to stop me, so I kept on going. They barked…a lot. They chased me and intimidated me to the best of their ability. Eventually, they just stopped and went back home. I could only think of one solution at the time. I had a friend at the end of the street, and I could ask her to play with me. The problem with this was that my friend had been mad at me, and we hadn't talked for weeks. To this day, I can't remember exactly why she was mad at me. I think I unintentionally said something insensitive when she was confiding in me about her newborn cousin who had medical issues. I was 10 years old, and I had no idea what I was supposed to say or not say about such a sensitive subject. Knowing she was mad at me; I decided to swallow my pride and see if she would forgive me and hang out.

I went to her door full of fear and my heart pounding. She said she had to do chores. This may have been true, but I highly doubted it at the time. The only other solution my fifth-grade mind could think of was to brave it out and go past the dogs again. After all, it worked the first time, and I could do it again.

As I rode back toward home, the dogs made another attempt to harm me. Once again, they barked, chased and intimidated. Only this time, one got in front of me, my front tire hit him, and I fell to the ground. The other dog took the opportunity to grab a hold of my head with his teeth.

I kicked and screamed. I remember seeing a third dog that lived next door to me. That dog's owner was my babysitter from time to time, so he knew me well. I have no doubt that he played a part in saving my life. I could hear him barking and imagined that he bit the other dog's tail or something because eventually, the dog attacking me decided to let go. I stood up and screamed as loud as I could, hoping someone would come running outside to my rescue, but also because I was so angry about what had just taken place.

I ran to the nearest door, which was the owner of the attacking dogs. He said, "Did my dogs do that?"

Between sobs and with a great deal of anger that probably did not come out in my young voice, I said, "Yes!"

I was so angry that this man was so irresponsible with his dogs, and I wanted him to see what they had done. He did what he could to help me. He brought me to his bathroom and put a cold, wet towel on my face and went to call my parents.

My dad was on his way out of the subdivision. He saw my bike lying in the middle of the road. He was panicked, thinking that I had been kidnapped. Then, he saw my mom running up the street in her house slippers. They loaded me up in the car and took me to the hospital, where they cleaned my wounds and gave my parents instructions for care at home. I had sustained four puncture wounds on my right cheek, a couple on the back of my head, one inside my ear and one on my shoulder.

Everyone was so nice to me for several weeks after the dog-bite incident. Our pastor came to our house to visit me. My friend forgave me and started talking to me again. I got student of the month for the second time in one school year.

The dog owners gave me a little locket and offered to pay any medical bills resulting from the incident. This was very kind of them, but dynamics started to change over time.

A few months after the incident, the wife told me how sad she felt because they had to put the dog that practically killed me to sleep. I didn't realize at the time that she was trying to make me feel guilty for something I had no control over, and that was no fault of my own. They should have kept a closer eye on their dangerous dogs and made sure they stayed inside their fence.

About a month or two later, the other dog killed an innocent kitten in the subdivision. Both events were very traumatizing for the entire neighborhood. The trauma still exists for me today. I'm not much of a dog person, and if I see a dog's teeth, I feel pressure on my face where my wounds were.

# Kids Are My Business

*See that you do not look down on one of these little ones. For I tell you that their angels in heaven always see the face of my Father in heaven.*
*-Matthew 18:10 NIV*

I have always loved babies, and I imagine I always will. When I was little, my friends and I spent hours playing with dolls and building houses out of blankets and lawn furniture. I would make up lullabies to sing to my baby dolls.

One summer, I was visiting my grandpa's auto body shop, and he had several kittens running around. I spent the days chasing the kittens and holding them. My goal was to get one to fall asleep in my arms, but I was not successful.

In the first grade, my class and I read a story about an abandoned baby. We read that the baby was soiled and smelled really bad. I thought, "I don't care; I'd still take that baby. I'd clean her up and take care of her."

One year, we had family from Alabama visit for my grandfather's 70th surprise birthday party. We had about eight people stay with us for a few days in our three-bedroom house. One of those visitors was a tiny baby, about three months old. I loved having a baby in my home day and night. I watched her mom boil bottles and observed all the things that went into taking care of a baby. It never occurred to me that it was a lot of work. It didn't seem like work to me.

I longed to have a baby living in our home. I'd be envious anytime I saw babies in public. I thought the parents and siblings were so lucky to always have them around at home to snuggle and play with at any time. I thought about how much fun it would be to take them on vacations. Every wish I made as a child was for a baby sister. However, my parents started their family later in life, so another baby was out of the question.

As I got older, my passion for babies led to work. At one point, I owned a sweatshirt that said, "Kids Are My Business." That has always been the case for me. Before I was old enough to babysit, I'd visit babies in my neighborhood and help by entertaining them while their moms got stuff done around the house. I had my first babysitting job when I was 12 years old. The children were six months old and five years old. This babysitting job was a big deal for me. I carried the baby everywhere, and after I got her to bed, I played board games and had a dance party with her big sister. I loved being in charge, not for the power but for the short-term responsibility for these young kids' safety and happiness. I babysat those girls about once a month until I graduated from high school.

I also spent a great deal of time with a family who lived at the end of my street. They had four children in a span of five years. One of the children had autism. It was my first experience with autism. Little did I know, I would have a child with the same diagnosis one day. I loved him and his siblings as well as their parents. One summer, I went to Disney World with them, followed by a few days at a beautiful beach resort. Strange as it may seem, I loved waking up to the noise and chaos every day. That vacation was one of my favorite trips of all time.

# Later Childhood to Adolescence

I went to week-long summer camps every year, starting when I was in the third grade. I'm glad my parents sent me to camp because I think it was good for me and made me more independent. However, I did not like it at the time. I had fun, but I was terribly homesick. I would wake up each day, counting down the days until it was time to go home.

One camp was not far away, and I fought the urge to walk home. The four girls in my tent were extremely homesick, and it made me feel worse. They cried every day and had nothing but negative things to say. When my parents got there to pick me up, I ran to them in tears, begging them not to send me back.

Summer camp was different the summer after I finished 7th grade. Childhood had quickly given way to adolescence. There was a girl in my cabin with beautiful hair that reminded me of Alicia Silverstone in the movie *Clueless* and Aerosmith's music video, *Cryin'*. I envied this girl at camp, not only because of her hair but because she had a boyfriend. The couple always sat by each other, held hands and laughed together. The thought of having a boyfriend had never occurred to me before, but after seeing the fun those two were having, I wanted a boyfriend of my own.

The other girls who were staying in my cabin wanted to help me get my first boyfriend. One of the girls had a brother who was at camp too. One night, the girls and I drafted a letter telling him I liked him. His sister gave us all sorts of information about his likes. The girl writing the letter told him I liked bands like Metallica, figuring he would want me to be his girlfriend if we had similar interests. I think he saw right through it because the letter didn't work. It was my first experience being rejected by a boy. This marked the beginning of my "boy crazy" years.

In the spring of my 8th grade year, I got a trampoline for my birthday, which was probably the best gift I have ever gotten. It was good for me because I stopped thinking about boys and was more interested in jumping on my new trampoline.

That summer, I'd go outside right after breakfast, spending hours perfecting my back layouts and front tucks. I'd go inside for a little while to cool off or get a snack and then go right back out. This went on for weeks. I felt like a kid again and was carefree.

I had forgotten all about boys until my brother brought a new friend home one day, Ben. He was funny and gave me attention. None of my brother's friends ever paid any attention to me before. Ben was different. We seemed to hit it off from day one. He asked me to be his girlfriend, and I happily agreed.

Having a boyfriend before being able to drive was not an easy task. The only time I really saw Ben was when he and my brother's roller hockey team had games. We broke up by the fall but remained friends.

Ben was different from the other boys in high school. I'd have boyfriends come and go, but Ben was always there. We'd talk on the phone, watch movies and just hang out. It was a friendship that lasted throughout my high school years.

I had a small but close group of friends during adolescence. My best friend was Annie. We spent nearly every waking moment on the phone with each other if we weren't together in person. We dressed and talked alike. We liked the same things. We knew each other more than we knew ourselves. I liked nothing more than to have sleepovers with Annie. We would watch movies, talk about boys, and eat junk food. Our favorite indulgences were brownies, Doritos, and Mountain Dew. We would talk until we fell asleep and resume conversation as soon as we woke up.

Annie and I enjoyed going to the mall. We also loved going to the state fair and other carnivals. Our all-time favorite ride was the Zipper. I loved the feeling of my stomach dropping. I can still hear Annie's low, raspy scream with each drop and spin of the ride.

When we could not be together, Annie and I would sit on the phone watching MTV music videos or shows like *Real World* and *Road Rules*. Sadly, by senior year, Annie and I drifted apart. We let boys get in between us and ended high school not talking.

After college, I had dreams about Annie that seemed so real. I would wake up painfully missing her and her companionship. Around that time, social media came around. I was able to find her there. We exchanged a few messages, but that was it.

One day, I was browsing social media and found a post stating Annie had suddenly died at the young age of 28. At first, I thought it was some sort of prank. Annie and I knew each other during our "invincible years." She still seemed immortal to me. After seeing more postings, I realized it was clearly no joke. I started to cry because in that moment, I lost all hope that we would have a friendship again on this Earth. Plus, knowing she was no longer in the world, living her life broke my heart.

I still think of Annie often. I'm still filled with nostalgia when I see the Zipper. I can't have a bite of Cocoa Puffs cereal without thinking about her. I hope to pick up where we left off in heaven one day.

While Annie and I were best friends, we had a group of other friends we often hung out with. Kayla lived near me, and Jennifer lived near Annie. Kayla and Jennifer were best friends too. The four of us were my core group. We'd hang out with a larger group at birthday parties, sleepovers and school.

There were many things my friends and I did as we were growing up that I am not proud of, but there is one thing that I will always regret. We were obsessed with knowing what the future held for us and turned to fortune-telling. It was very addictive yet always left us feeling unsatisfied…a sign that the devil was at work in us. I have since asked God for forgiveness for using fortune-telling of any kind. Today, I avoid it at all costs and encourage others to do the same. I even stay away from horoscopes and want no part of Magic 8 Balls.

*Trust in the Lord with all your heart and lean not on your own understanding; in all your ways acknowledge him, and he will make your paths straight. – Proverbs 3:5-6 NIV*

As my friends and I made our way through high school, our friendships changed and eventually came to an end. I seemed to get boy crazy before the other girls in my social group. I had boyfriend after boyfriend and preferred their company over my friends. Looking back, I wish I hadn't done that because my friends were always happy to be with me, but boyfriends lasted an average of five weeks and then they were gone leaving me heartbroken. My friends were satisfying gifts from God.

Boyfriends threw me into a vicious unhealthy cycle of daydreaming. I constantly felt empty, and the daydreaming was really impacting my grades. Instead of listening to the teachers and taking notes, I would sit and think about interactions with boys that had either happened or that I wished would happen.

During my sophomore year of high school, I met Neal. He was stout with dark brown eyes and brown skin. His parents were born and raised in India. I did not like Neal at first, but he sure liked me. He was very persistent. Neal grew on me, and we ended up dating for a year and a half. After about a year, tables turned, and I was obsessed with him, and he started backing off.

One day I started crying when we were outside my house, and I told him it felt like he did not "love" me anymore. Instead of reassuring me, he yelled at me and told me that his failures were all my fault. This should have been the end of that relationship, but it went on for six more miserable months. Neal ended up going to college during my senior year in high school.

Senior year was likely the most miserable year of my life. While my relationship with Neal was crumbling, my friends were in serious relationships of their own. Every lunch period, I ate quietly as I listened to all the intimate details about my friends' relationships. There were no longer large sleepovers or get-togethers. Annie and I barely spoke anymore. Kayla and I were constantly getting into petty arguments which were likely my fault. At the time, I was so irritable and took everything personally. Kayla was always quick to forgive and really valued our friendship.

I spent nearly every night alone doing homework and studying. I usually fell asleep waiting for Neal to call. I just wanted things to be back to the way they were with him, but I realized it would never happen.

One day at lunch, as one of my friends divulged a rather detailed story about her and her boyfriend, I excused myself and went to the library. With shaking hands and my heart beating out of my chest, I drafted a break-up email to Neal and clicked send.

After my break-up with Neal, I had a clearer mind since I was no longer wondering about our future. My friends were all busy with their boyfriends. I didn't dare give them a hard time about it because I spent the prior three years ditching *them* for boys.

I started talking to Andrea a lot in history class, and we became good friends. Andrea had a boyfriend who was a junior. One night, we went to her boyfriend's friend's house, where I met Eddie. In the back of my mind, I knew my mom wanted me to go to my senior prom. I hated prom and homecoming, but she thought I would have fun and would regret it if I didn't go.

I thought Eddie would be an acceptable person to go to prom with, even though he was a junior. Eddie and I became a couple, admittedly because it was the month of April, and I needed a prom date. Eddie was very kind and would have given me the world if he could, but I really had no desire for a boyfriend. I was still mourning the loss of Neal and regrouping from his emotional abuse. The night before prom, Neal called me and made me feel bad about going to prom with someone other than him, not that he wanted to go with me.

Prom night was a horrible night for me. Eddie kept putting his hand on my waist, and I kept pushing it off. I'm not sure why he didn't get the hint. Neal kept paging me on my purple pager. I guess he wanted to make sure I wasn't having too much fun without him. My original group of friends and I were not on speaking terms. I was hanging out with a crowd younger than me, aside from Andrea, who kept disappearing.

I ended up crying in the bathroom at one point, but with the help of a peer, I concluded that none of it was going to matter in the months and years to come. I was moving on and making a new life for myself. Soon enough, high school would be a distant memory. After realizing this, I regained composure and went back to my date.

Shortly after, we left for a party at a junior's home. It was a nice party, but I felt out of place being a senior. I didn't even know where Andrea was at that point. I asked Eddie to take me home early, and I slept most of the next day. I would have been much happier in my pajamas watching movies all night. Large crowds and parties are not my thing.

Graduation came shortly after prom night. Kayla and I made up and were on speaking terms again, but most of my other friends, including Annie, went their separate ways. Before Neal and I had broken up, I chose to enroll in the same college as him, Southern Illinois University at Edwardsville (SIUE). I had a glimmer of hope that Neal and I would get back together in college.

The summer after graduation was quiet. Ben and I hung out some. I had a daytime babysitting job and worked in retail in evenings and on weekends. Andrea and Kayla were basically my only friends. Later that summer, I found out Neal was not going to SIUE in the fall. I was devastated but little did I know, someone much better, a true gift from God was going to come along in the very near future.

# College/ Young Adulthood

Moving into the dorms at SIUE was very memorable. I was standing in line at the University Center with my parents and all the other freshmen and their parents. I was eager to make friends and have a fresh start. My first friend in college was Riley. She was very friendly and introduced herself to me as we waited to get the keys to our dorms. As fate would have it, Riley and I were on the same floor and wing. She stayed a few doors down the hall from me.

Making friends in college was much easier than I thought it would be. Riley and I became close with a couple of other girls right away. Within a week, we became friends with a couple of guys. Jake was one of the guys. He was over a foot taller than me and had dark hair and light skin. We walked to class together every morning. I don't remember what we talked about, but we were never at a loss for words, and it never got romantic. It was refreshing. Jake helped me begin to see that there are good guys out there who are mature and treat girls with respect. He seemed to enjoy my company. He valued my opinion and never put me down.

I've always liked structured time such as class and organized activities. Finding things to do during my free time has always caused a bit of anxiety for me. A group of us would go to aerobics together on campus and I really enjoyed that. My friends and I weren't really the partying type, but we thought it was a must in college. We went to a couple of parties near campus but never drank a whole lot. Riley had a cousin who went to college at Mizzou, which had a lot more parties than SIUE. One weekend, we took a road trip with a couple of other girls to Mizzou.

At Mizzou, we went to the kind of parties I had seen in movies. There were parties held in garages with kegs and crowds of people. There were parties that stretched over an entire block with different houses participating. It was neat to see, but nobody in my group got into the drinking. We had enough to make us feel sick to our stomachs but no buzz or anything. I never understood the hype because that was typically how drinking went for me.

Instead of partying, I had a lot more fun hanging out with my friends without alcohol. Riley was from a suburb of St. Louis. She would take me across the river to her favorite mall. She introduced me to Lion's Choice roast beef sandwiches and Krispy Kreme donuts. We visited her home a couple of times as well. I liked going to her house. It was nestled in a quiet neighborhood. Her mom was pleasant to talk with. It just felt comforting to be there.

I loved my time with Riley and our friends, but I longed to have another boyfriend. I didn't want an unhealthy relationship like I had in high school. I didn't want to be used or have my heart broken again.

I was able to formulate exactly what I wanted in a relationship, and I asked God for help. I prayed that He would bless me with someone who could not get enough of me and vice versa. Little did I know, my prayer was about to be answered.

*You can pray for anything, and if you have faith, you will receive it.*
*-Matthew 21:22 NLT*

Late September of my Freshman year in college, my friend Jennifer from high school invited me and a couple of my new friends over for a get-together. Jennifer moved to Highland, Illinois during our high school years. Jennifer and I had gotten closer when we were in a science class together before she had to move.

Jennifer was not afraid to be herself. She did not seem to feel the need to conform. She had older siblings which may be why she always seemed to have more wisdom than the rest of us. I was very sad when I heard she had to move because her dad's job had relocated. Thankfully, Highland is only a 30-minute drive from SIUE, so we got together quite a bit in college.

Shortly before I went to the gathering at Jennifer's, she told me that a friend she met at a local community college might be stopping by. His name was Brandon. Jennifer said he may bring a friend too. She was very clear that she liked Brandon, and she wanted to become more than friends with him.

Brandon and his friend stopped by to drop some school notes off to Jennifer. Brandon says he got one glimpse of me and decided to stay. It was love at first sight. Throughout the evening, he kept asking Jennifer about me and how he could ask me out. Jennifer then would come to me disgruntled, telling me what he had said. I assured her that I would not go out with him since she liked him. I was more interested in Brandon's friend, but he was in a relationship, so I had no business even looking at him.

A few hours and drinks later (not that I was drunk or even buzzed), we all ended up in the basement. Brandon's friend was sitting next to me on the couch. Brandon was on the floor with puppy dog eyes and eventually went upstairs. For some reason, I was drawn to him, heartbroken over the puppy dog eyes.

The group of us found spots in the living room to crash for the night. I took the spot next to Brandon on the floor. Jennifer was on the other side of him on the couch. The windows were open, and the fresh fall air flowed through the room.

The next morning, Jennifer and I had a brief discussion, and she very graciously gave me her blessing to move forward with Brandon. Like a saint, Jennifer remained very supportive of me and Brandon.

The day after the party, I was in familiar territory. I was replaying the night over and over in my head. I wondered how long it would be until Brandon called me. Would he play hard to get and wait a few days like most boys did? Would he even call me at all?

Much to my surprise, Brandon called me before noon! Plus, he told me that he missed me. I was shocked. No boy had ever been that vulnerable with me, much less so soon. I think most girls would have run in the opposite direction. It would have scared them to have someone so forward. But not me. I gladly took him into my life. He was the answer to my prayer.

My life started taking a turn after meeting Brandon. Parties gave way to dates and time with family. One evening, I went to dinner with my grandparents who lived near campus. I told them all about Brandon, none of us realizing that Brandon would be a part of our family one day or that they would absolutely love him. He would fit right in and make them laugh on numerous occasions. Brandon was not only the answer to my prayer, but he was what I needed. Before meeting Brandon, I was not sure who I was. Like many new college students, I was floundering trying to figure that out.

Brandon and I had so much fun together, just the two of us. He would come and get me on Fridays after my last class of the week and drive me to the St. Louis area. Like my time with Riley, we would go shopping and out to eat at places I had never been like Fitz's and Blueberry Hill. One day, my small group of friends and I were hanging out, and the conversation went to Brandon. One person said they saw Brandon and I dancing out in the rain. They were envious of how happy and in love we were.

I didn't doubt Brandon's love for me. I was confident he enjoyed being with me just as much as I enjoyed being with him. We talked on the phone daily. He would always tell me how he felt. He wasn't one to act weird or distant like the guys in my past did. My college years would have gone in a much different direction if it weren't for Brandon. He was God's gift given to me at the most perfect time.

*Then the Lord God said, "It is not good for the man to be alone. I will make a helper who is just right for him." -Genesis 2:18 NLT*

# Working in Daycare

As my freshman year of college came to an end, I began to look for summer work. I moved back home with my parents that summer. Working was not a new thing for me. I worked in retail my last couple of years in high school and on Christmas vacation and spring break during my freshman year of college. I knew I wanted a change though. I never really liked retail. I hated standing on my feet for eight hours, dealing with rude customers and bossy coworkers. I don't know why I didn't think of it sooner, but I decided to apply to local daycare centers.

My first daycare job was at a large center in Springfield. It was my dream job at the time. I was a floater teacher for infants and toddlers. I worked four 10-hour days, covering the days off for teachers in four different classrooms. Before I started my job, I had a conversation with my mom about toddlers. I asked, "What age are toddlers?"

My mom was not sure either but assumed they were 2 and 3-year-olds. Much to our surprise, they were 15-24 months old. Still babies but transitioning to walking, talking little children. I loved them! There was a lot of crying though. In fact, I would hear each one of their little cries in my mind as I went to sleep at night.

I loved to nurture them, play toys with them, do arts and crafts, and take them outside or to the indoor gym. I loved patting their little backs as they laid on their cots at naptime and watching their eyes involuntarily close as they drifted off to sleep. It was a piece of heaven on Earth for me. Little did I know, it was a glimpse of what I would experience with my own children in the years to come.

Shortly after returning to college for my sophomore year, I was out to get another job. I wanted to continue working with little ones in a daycare setting. There was a church that was opening a new daycare, and I applied at the right time. They liked my daycare experience and hired me as they opened the new business. The daycare started out small but grew quickly. The center started to feel like home, and the children and staff were like family.

I started out working in the infant room. My coworkers were a mix of new moms and fellow college students. My coworkers and I grew close because there were not many of us, and we worked with each other frequently. We talked about school and wedding plans. We often hung out at each other's apartments after work.

By my junior year of college, I worked my way up to the assistant director of the daycare. I would open the doors at 6:00 AM and spend the morning hours there. By the time I got to my first afternoon class, I was tired. Thankfully, my Geology teacher didn't say a thing the few times I dozed off in class.

There was one lady who I worked with that really made an impression on me, Sarah. She reminds me a lot of myself now. Sarah and I worked in the infant room together for quite a while. Her son also happened to be one of the infants. At the time, I didn't understand the magnitude of love between mothers and their babies. Sarah was always so happy to be with her son, even when he was fussy. She sang to him and snuggled him. I'll admit I was annoyed because this often took her away from helping with the other babies, but she tried her best. Sarah had four children at the time I knew her. I imagine she has had more by now. She was such a wonderful mother. She and her husband took their children to church regularly. I am certain this woman had joy and help from God.

# Living Alone

I had my own apartment during my last year and a half of college. I experienced the dorm life and spent a year living in the on-campus apartments, but having my own place was by far the best living situation for me. I woke up early to open the daycare center. When I was not working, I was often studying. I took college very seriously. I wasn't the best student in high school, but all the solitude during my senior year of high school allowed me time to improve my study skills which helped me tackle my college coursework. I can't say the public school I attended prepared me for college. When it came down to it, it was the study skills I figured out myself that prepared me.

Looking back on my years living alone, I realize how easy I had it. I knew at the time that it was a great life. On a typical day when I didn't have plans with Brandon or friends, I'd finish a fulfilling day of work and school and make something simple for dinner when I got home. Then, I would go for a walk or bike ride. I'd settle down with some studying. Then, fall asleep watching *Flintstones* or *Dawson's Creek* DVDs which were gifts from Brandon.

I loved that I could come home from work or school and unwind by myself. I didn't have to worry about roommates staying up late when I had to go to work early in the morning. I could go to bed and wake up as early as I wanted.

I slept in until about 9:00 AM on Saturdays and spent most of the day studying and doing my laundry. I remember feeling like I accomplished so much by doing laundry for one. These years prepared me for my future. I had to learn how to take care of myself before I could take care of others. I was happy during this time in my life, but I wouldn't go back if I had the choice.

While I had my own apartment, Brandon was still living at his parent's house in their basement, about 30 minutes away. He was respectful of my time and place and didn't hang around my apartment too often. We primarily stuck to our daily phone calls, midweek visits, and weekend dates. Brandon proposed to me in 2003. We decided to have a long engagement and get married on our five-year anniversary, September 24th, 2005.

During my senior year of college, I was accepted into a master's program at University of Illinois Springfield. Brandon and I decided to find an apartment in Springfield and move in together. Living together before marriage is not something I would do now, nor is it something I would recommend for anyone.  I know now that it is not something God approves of. This was a time in our lives that Brandon and I did not seek or follow God. You will see in later chapters that eventually, things started spiraling out of control as a result.

# Part 2: Life Our Way

# Our Wedding

Having a long engagement meant a lot of anticipation, but there was plenty of wedding planning to do during that time. I had no idea how much was involved in planning a wedding. Invitations, guest list, menu, venues, photography, flowers, decorations, finding a dress, music and the list goes on.

During the early planning stages, we came across a wedding invitation with a picture of a young boy giving a little girl a flower. It was a perfect theme for us. The wedding was in the beginning of fall 2005, so we also wanted to incorporate fall colors.

Normally, I wouldn't have put much thought or effort on flowers, but I won some arrangements by entering a drawing at a wedding planning event. The florist called me, congratulating me for winning and invited me to her home to look at her prior work.

Picking out flowers was a bit overwhelming. It didn't help that I had the worst case of laryngitis I have ever had. I could barely squeak any words out, but the florist didn't seem to mind. She patiently waited as I quietly looked through her photo albums. Doing this, I discovered my favorite flower...gerbera daisies. I loved the various colors for our fall theme like dark purple, orange, and yellow. The session with the florist really helped me begin to see a vision for the wedding.

Another memorable part of wedding planning was finding a dress. My mom, bridesmaids, and Brandon's mom went with me for this crucial occasion. For my body type, I wanted a dress that was full in the bottom to cover my thighs and form-fitting on the top to accentuate my torso. I tried on a few before finding the perfect one. The dress had a lot of detail including lace and pearls over the entire garment. It was held up by a strap behind my neck and about ten thin straps fanning down each side of my back. I couldn't wait for Brandon to see it on our wedding day.

After what seemed like forever, the day had arrived. My four bridesmaids and I slept at a hotel the night before. Many of our out-of-town guests stayed at the same hotel. It had been raining the week leading up to the wedding, so I was a bit nervous about the weather. I was elated when we went outside that morning, and the sun was shining. I must have shouted some sort of statement of elation because

Brandon's relatives started cheering right along with me. It was a great start to the day.

After getting our hair and make-up done at a salon, we arrived at the church. My bridesmaids and I went to the church's nursery to get ready. This may seem like an odd choice of room, but the attached bathroom came in handy for finishing touches on hair and makeup. The toys and books were good for the kids who were in the wedding.

We were all completely ready and waiting for the ceremony to begin when my little ring bearer started getting restless. I knew my ring bearer from daycare. He and I bonded so much that I asked for him to be in my wedding. As we both grew tired of waiting, I suggested we read a book. The activity was familiar and calming for both of us.

The time had come to walk down the aisle. I anxiously wrapped my arm around my dad's, and we headed toward Brandon. As I watched Brandon wipe a tear away from his eye, I choked back tears of my own. When Brandon and I exchanged our vows, I had a great deal of hope and excitement for our future. I was in awe of the 200 guests that had come to see our special day. Some of the guests were young married couples that we had witnessed get married. It seemed so unreal that it was finally our turn.

During the wedding planning process, we had carefully selected music that best described our relationship and feelings for each other. We had a slide show of photos played to the song of *Home to Me* by Josh Kelley. As we lit the unity candle, a friend sang *Making Memories of Us* by Keith Urban.

Before I knew it, the ceremony was over, and Brandon and I walked out of the room as husband and wife as all our friends and family rejoiced. After the guests had left and started making their way to the reception hall, we had a lot of photos taken. I was growing weary and eager to get to our guests at the reception. Kayla reminded me that I would be thankful we got all the pictures, and she was right.

After the indoor pictures, we all loaded up in a limo bus and headed to my mom's favorite landmark, a local covered bridge located behind my childhood home. It was the perfect location for outdoor photos. My favorite photo was of me, Brandon and our wedding party jumping in the air as we locked arms.

Once the photos were finally complete, we headed to the reception hall. The DJ announced our names and we walked in the room as everyone cheered. We took our seats and listened to some heart-felt toasts before having dinner.

Brandon and I danced our first dance as husband and wife to *More than Love* by Los Lonely Boys. We had spent months preparing a special but not over-the-top dance for our guests. We had a lot of fun practicing as well as performing.

After the special dances, traditional bouquet/garter toss and cake cutting, we danced the night away. We had so much fun with our friends and family. I was so relaxed and ready to celebrate everything going so smoothly. My favorite song played at the reception was *Sweet Caroline* by Neil Diamond. Brandon and I sang at the top of our lungs with our wedding party as they played that song.

After our reception, Brandon and I went back to our apartment to wait for our ride to the airport which was scheduled to arrive early in the morning. We had an entire day of travel ahead of us, but we were excited for our honeymoon in Curacao which is a tiny island by Aruba. We got the destination idea from friends of ours who got married a week after our return.

The wedding may have gone without a hitch, but our travel was another story. We spent the entire day on an airplane. Our last connection flight was in San Juan. It was a tiny airplane…a puddle jumper. My nerves grew even more intense when I noticed the airsick bags were more abundant and accessible than they were on our prior flights. As Brandon and I were discussing our concerns about this plane, we were informed that our flight was cancelled due to the air traffic control tower being down in Curacao.

We were crushed, but the airline set us up at a beautiful resort in San Juan for the evening. They gave us a food voucher that was enough to cover two buffet meals at the resort. However, we had never eaten any of the food that was on the buffet, nor were we in the mood to experiment with new tastes. Instead, we enjoyed chicken strips and fries on our room's balcony with a lovely view of the ocean. We were sulking a bit about the change in plans. To this day, we regret not making the most of it and taking a walk on the beach or going for a swim.

The next day, we boarded a normal-size plane in San Juan, only to fly up to Florida and then back down to Curacao. It seemed counter-productive, but we were willing to do anything to get to our honey-moon destination.

Once we arrived, we were relieved but also a little nervous. Curacao did not look like a safe place to be as we rode the shuttle to our resort. However, once we got to the resort, we felt a lot safer and vowed to not leave during our stay.

There was plenty to do at the resort to keep us busy. There were restaurants and excursions. We spent most of the time lying by the ocean and cooling off in the waves. We watched tiny crabs pop out of the sand, quickly crawl sideways and then go back down into the sand. I was terrified that I was going to accidentally step on one. There were also a lot of lizards. In fact, one morning a lizard crawled right on my plate and ate a piece of leftover fruit.

The last night of our honeymoon was the most memorable. There was a special dinner event set up on the beach. Our table was as close as you can get to the ocean without being swept into the water. We were so happy to be together and to be married. We were sad our honeymoon was almost over but excited to get home and get my driver's license changed with my new name and get a joint checking account. We were ready to tackle this life together for the long run.

*Two are better than one, because they have a good return for their work: If one falls down, his friend can help him up. But pity the man who falls and has no one to help him up! Also, if two lie down together, they will keep warm. But how can one keep warm alone? Though one may be overpowered, two can defend themselves. A cord of three strands is not quickly broken. -Ecclesiastes 4:9-12 NIV*

# Marriage Before Kids

As newlyweds, we lived in the same apartment we had been in the year prior. It felt different though. Brandon and I were thrilled to call each other husband and wife. We had a schedule that allowed for a smooth transition combining our separate lives into one.

Brandon had a typical Monday through Friday daytime job. My schedule was less typical. I often had a few hours of free time in the morning, worked a few hours in the afternoon, and then went to graduate school in the evening. Brandon had most evenings to play video games or watch TV. I used my solo morning hours to workout and unwind.

Step aerobics was my favorite form of exercise. I attended a class regularly, working out with people much older than me, many of them retired. Step aerobics made me feel coordinated. It was an energizing and fulfilling workout.

After aerobics, I'd go home to shower and eat a semi-healthy lunch while I watched my favorite show at the time called *Starting Over*. It was a show about life coaches helping people with mental health or crisis issues. It taught me a lot for my field of study which was counseling.

Brandon and I spent as much time together as possible when I wasn't in class or studying. We often sat out on our back porch and talked. One time we tried to go for a run together but ended up laughing too much so we had to walk instead. We liked to order pizza and watch movies on one of the few weeknights we had together. On Saturday mornings, we slept in and watched cartoons as we ate breakfast. We kept our dating schedule up and went out for dinner about once a week.

Brandon and I hung out with friends a few times a month. We did most of our socializing with other couples. Most of us did not have children at the time, so no need for babysitters. Of course, Brandon and I were happy to have kids in tow if our friends had them. We usually went out to dinner and then went back to each other's homes to play games and just talk. We didn't text our friends back then. If we wanted to talk, we simply called them.

Life seemed challenging to us at the time with bills, jobs, and school papers. Little did we know, those were probably the easiest years of our lives. We had each other, good health, our youth, and very few responsibilities.

Occasionally, I would babysit, and Brandon would always be willing to come along to spend time with me and the kids. We worked well together. He was the fun one, and I was the nurturer. I can't remember one disagreement we had while babysitting; an indication we would be a great parenting team one day.

Despite my love for children, I didn't really think about having kids of my own until after my first year of marriage. A friend of mine from high school who was one year younger than me told me at work that she was pregnant. She had the biggest smile when she told me. I was filled with curiosity. I asked her how she felt. I wanted to know every little detail. A short time after I had found out my friend was pregnant, I told Brandon I wanted to start trying to have a baby. It caught him a bit off guard at first because we hadn't really talked about having our own children anytime soon. I had been so busy taking care of everyone else's children and finishing graduate school, I didn't ever feel a strong yearning for my own until then. Brandon had to give some thought to this major life-change, but he was on board a week or two later.

I became immersed in pregnancy information. I joined groups online and read all about young women's journeys into motherhood. I analyzed my monthly cycles and symptoms. I was sure I was pregnant in November 2006, but I wasn't. Ridiculously, I thought since we had one failed month, one of us was infertile.

In December 2006, I was very busy finishing up my Master's thesis. It was a trying time of meeting with the department's lead professor when it was most convenient for him, often having to wait outside his office because he was never on time or forgot our appointment all together. He was never apologetic for making me wait as if his time was more precious than mine. I've experienced this many times since then with people who hold some sort of power. It was my first taste of this annoyance in life. Every time we did meet, my professor would have about seven small Post-it notes with suggested corrections running down every page. I'd make the corrections, and he'd have seven more Post-its per page the next time. This had been going on for months.

One weekend, Brandon spent hours helping me put the finishing touches on the project and getting the margins just right. I was so frustrated and tired that tears ran down my face. I realized that I had been a little extra emotional lately, but I chalked it up to stress. I just wanted to be done with school and move on to motherhood and my career.

My thesis was complete, and I officially graduated from graduate school at the end of December 2006. I immediately started a new job doing casework in the child welfare field. One day, I went for a morning workout before going to work. As I ran on the indoor track, I felt a little sluggish, but I attributed it to eating too many Christmas sweets. I pushed myself to run harder to work off those extra calories. By the time my workout was over, I noticed some cramping. Then, I recalled I had been waking up sweating the last few mornings, which was unusual for me. Even still, I brushed this all aside and headed to work.

The next morning, I woke up sweating again. Brandon was already at work, but I couldn't wait to find out what was going on. I tore open a pregnancy test. Sure enough, there were two lines. I was pregnant! I was in complete disbelief. I jumped up and down and thanked God. Then, I began to worry that jumping would hurt the baby, so I stopped.

My first pregnancy was easy. I did not feel sick at all. I did have gestational diabetes, which resulted in me doing insulin shots. I had to go to the doctor frequently toward the end, but I loved seeing my growing baby on the ultrasounds. Pregnancy was such a new and unique experience.

# *Logan*

One evening in August 2007, Brandon and I went out to eat with my mom and dad. It was a celebration dinner. It was my parent's anniversary. Plus, I was going to the hospital that same night to be induced. I was very pregnant and caught the eye of nearly everyone at the restaurant. My dad made a comment about everyone looking at my belly. It was something I had noticed over the last few months as I had started showing. I'll admit, my eyes are often drawn to pregnant bellies as well. I think about the precious little baby in the room that cannot be seen. The little life inside the mom's belly. It's such a miracle!

After dinner, Brandon and I said our goodbyes to my parents and made our way to the hospital. I was so excited and nervous. Once we got into our hospital room, I marveled at the little bassinet sitting near my bed. It seemed so surreal to think that my baby was going to be in that bassinet in the very near future. I couldn't wait! However, it was a much longer wait than we anticipated.

The first night, they administered Cervidil, which is supposed to ripen the cervix. It didn't work the first night, so they tried again the next. I was comfortable the whole time. Brandon and I watched movies and just hung out in the hospital room.

The second round of Cervidil did not work either. My doctor broke my water, but things still weren't progressing. After 48 hours, not much had changed. I told my doctor I was ready for a c-section. The main reason I opted for a c-section was there was meconium in my fluid which told me Logan was not doing one hundred percent in there. I was just ready to have him in my arms, safe and sound.

Around 7:30 PM, I became a mom for the first time. My thoughts after having Logan surprised me. First, I thought, "He's perfect!" My second thought, "I don't want to do that."

I was so wrapped up in the pregnancy that I didn't think about being responsible for a tiny human 24 hours a day. I had forgotten about how much I'd dreamt about this day as a young child. I was also exhausted and pumped full of medication I'd never been on before, and I just wanted to take a nap.

The feeling of dread quickly subsided when they handed me my newborn baby. The nurse told me that I was the only one who could hold my baby as they rolled us to our room. It was the first time I felt a sense of importance as a mother. I looked forward to those strolls with each of my newborns.

I had spent nearly my whole life helping take care of other people's babies. I simply could not believe I had a baby of my own. Brandon heard me say several times that I could not believe Logan was ours. I was filled with joy and fear in equal amounts.

On our last night at the hospital, the cafeteria staff came to our room offering us freshly baked brownies. It was the best brownie of my life since I couldn't eat many sweets while pregnant because of gestational diabetes. After enjoying the brownie, the nurse realized how exhausted I was. Lack of sleep was very new to us. Brandon and I had spent years with uninterrupted sleep and going to bed and getting up when we wanted, aside from when we had to be up for work or other engagements. Logan wanted us to hold him constantly and was not fond of that little bed I had been staring at longingly while waiting for his arrival. This nurse understood how exhausted I was and offered to take Logan to the nursery for a couple of hours.

Brandon and I slept soundly until the nurse came back. I was woken up by the sound of a newborn crying. "Is that our baby?" I asked Brandon. I loved the sound of that… "our baby." It *was* our baby, and I was still so tired, but I didn't mind. I missed him even while I was sleeping, a new phenomenon that came with motherhood.

# Life with One Child

I quickly learned that having a child day in and day out is a lot different from having them eight hours at a daycare center. While on maternity leave, I would try to go for walks with Logan, and he would fuss. I would try to play with him, and he would fuss. I would get him down for a nap, and it maybe lasted a half hour or so. His fussing and crying pulled at my heartstrings every time, so I put in a lot of effort to keep him happy. By the end of the day, I was spent! Once he reached about six months, things got a lot better.

One weekend, Brandon went to visit a friend in Chicago while I stayed home with Logan. I had a lot of fun taking Logan to the train station to pick Brandon up. Little things like that were so enjoyable. I loved watching the wonder and excitement in his eyes. Everything was new to him.

Just about every spare moment I had, went to Logan. I could not get enough of him. I felt like I was forgetting something every time I dropped him off at daycare. It was a feeling I couldn't shake. I could not get to him fast enough at the end of the day. If I got off work early, I'd go straight to the daycare to get him. I finally understood those moms who would come to the daycare for thirty minutes on their lunch break to hold, breastfeed, or play with their little ones. I had become one of those moms.

As Logan reached a year old, I started feeling like I was ready for baby number two. Brandon was ready as well. We were surprised when I fell pregnant shortly after Logan's first birthday. The familiar look of those two lines on the pregnancy test was very exciting! Despite the gestational diabetes, I felt great during my pregnancy with Logan. I was ready to do it all over again. I couldn't wait to see the baby on the ultrasounds. I longed to feel the first kicks. I was so happy to be giving Logan a sibling.

Right around six weeks in, I started spotting. Sometimes that is normal, so I tried not to worry too much until I had an ultrasound. As Brandon and I watched the screen, we saw the tiny baby and a tiny heartbeat. However, we also saw my body contracting and trying to swoop the baby right out of my womb. The ultrasound tech did not seem to think it was promising. The doctor agreed and told me to take a week off work to rest.

The morning after my doctor's appointment, Brandon and I knew I had miscarried by the look of the blood loss I had. I cried...hard...like a baby. The emotional pain was immeasurable. The hopes and dreams I had for this baby since the moment I saw those two lines were gone, just like that.

I still took off that week the doctor had ordered. All I wanted to do was be with Logan during that time. I kept him out of daycare, and we spent most of those days cuddled on the couch, watching his favorite shows. As I held him close, I gazed at his little hands and feet. I realized this guy was an absolute miracle. I vowed to never take him or my future children for granted.

The baby I lost probably crosses my mind every day. We really don't know the gender of the baby, but we suspect it was a girl, and we named her Samantha Grace. It is just a name that popped in my head before we lost her. I imagine I will be meeting her in heaven one day, a moment I look forward to.

*Jesus said, "Let the little children come to me, and do not hinder them, for the kingdom of heaven belongs to such as these."*
*-Matthew 19:14 NIV*

# *Lily*

Shortly after my miscarriage, I became pregnant again. One day in church, I felt very tired. I couldn't keep my eyes open, which is a feeling I had while pregnant with Logan. We picked up a pregnancy test on the way home and were elated to see a positive result!

This pregnancy was much different from Logan's. Once I hit six weeks, I was incredibly nauseous, and that lasted a few months. There were nights I would wake up with my eyes watering from nearly being sick in my sleep. It was rough, but I took it as a sign that things were going well with the pregnancy. I was thrilled to find out at twenty weeks that I was having a girl! I called my mom right after the ultrasound to tell her, and I started crying tears of joy.

Lily was born in September, about a week before my scheduled c-section. One day I came home from work and told Brandon I just didn't feel right. I asked him to give Logan a bath, but I could see Brandon was tired from a long day at work, so I told him to go get his shower and ended up giving Logan his bath anyway. After bathtime, Logan and I went into the living room to play with toys. I knelt on an exercise ball and felt a gush of fluid. We called my parents to come over and watch Logan, and we headed to the hospital.

They did numerous tests and were about ready to send me home. Then, they did one last test. I could see the doctor and nurse exchanging glances, and I knew before they even told me that I wasn't going anywhere. They confirmed my water broke, and I was going to be meeting my baby girl very soon! I had the choice to attempt a regular birth with Lily but opted for another c-section after several hours had passed and things were not progressing.

Lily's hospital stay was much different from Logan's. I had packed all kinds of outfits, sleep gowns, blankets, and burp cloths. This time, I *knew* the baby was ours, and I wanted her to use all our belongings, not the hospital's stuff. I felt instantly bonded to Lily and figured out newborn babies just like to be held a lot.

Brandon and I didn't want Logan to have to spend the night without one of us, so I was by myself at the hospital each night. My friend, Courtney from college visited the first night. She made sure I had everything I needed close by to get through the night, like diapers and wipes. Throughout the night, I would feed Lily, burp her, and change her. We'd sleep and do it all over again. This wouldn't seem like much fun to most people, but it is one of my fondest memories. I was thrilled to be a mother to a second child but even more thrilled to have a girl. I loved Logan dearly, and I wanted him to be a boy before we found out he was, in fact, a boy. But there is something different about having a daughter. I can see myself in her. I can relate to her and her feelings because I've been there. Yet, she is different with a personality of her own.

Lily was a fun baby and young child. She was like my baby doll at first. I loved to dress her up. I carried her around everywhere I went throughout the house. The teachers at her daycare all loved her too. They would take her with them to do the laundry or random chores. One day when I came to pick her and Logan up, Lily's teacher showed me Lily's extraordinary artwork. It was an American flag. Lily did an excellent job following directions, and it turned out to be very similar to the sample. Logan still talks about how he remembers all the daycare teachers congregating around his sister's artwork.

One day, Lily didn't seem like she felt good. My mom was scheduled to be her babysitter that day while Brandon and I worked. Lily seemed so unwell that I advised my mom not to come. Brandon took off work to take care of her. As he was working in the kitchen, he heard her start to vomit. He rushed in to help her. She apologized, and he said, "That's ok; sometimes it just sneaks up on you."

Later that day as she was telling me what happened, she asked me if I knew that "Sometimes, it just sneaks up on you."

I laughed and confirmed with Brandon that he taught her that.

I felt so bad that she had gotten sick while I was at work and not there for her. I was terribly busy at work, but I took a couple of hours off to come home to help for a while.

When I got home, Lily looked very uncomfortable, and I knew she was going to get sick again. After the second episode, I thought she would want to lay down. Instead, she went to her closet. I watched her intently, wondering what she was doing. She brought out a board game to play with me. I guess she figured she would get some game time in with me since I was home from work in the middle of the day. I was impressed by her resilience.

Lily continues to keep busy. She is very good at trampoline and tumbling. She practices on a trampoline in our backyard just like I did, but has surpassed me by far. She gets nervous at gymnastics meets, so I got her a key chain with the following verse engraved on it. She keeps it on the bag that she takes to her meets.

*For I am the Lord, your God, who takes hold of your right hand and says to you, Do not fear; I will help you. -Isaiah 41:13 NIV*

# Lucian:
# Not the One in Our Family

After we had Lily, Brandon and I decided we were done with having children. We had the "perfect family"; one boy and one girl. Brandon has a sister, and I have a brother. We thought that was how it was supposed to be for our family too.

We were not making very much money at the time. My salary was barely enough to pay for daycare. We would often put daycare on the credit card just to make ends meet. With the financial stress and feeling like we had to do things just like our parents did, Brandon and I decided it was time for Brandon to get a vasectomy. We did not pray about it or ask for God's input before making the decision. At that time, we were running our lives the way we wanted or thought we should. I did not have a good feeling about it at all. Now, I realize that sense of uneasiness was a tug from God.

One morning, about a year after the vasectomy, I dropped the kids off at daycare. I stopped to look at the daily chart in Lily's classroom and took a step back. I didn't realize that there was a toddler sitting behind me, and I stepped right on him. I felt awful. The teacher consoled him. At that point, he wanted nothing to do with me, this stranger who just stepped on him. As the teacher was comforting him, I learned that this little boy's name was Lucian. My heart skipped a beat as I thought about how much I liked that name, Lucian. That would be a perfect name for a third baby, but I thought we would never have a third baby because of the vasectomy. Still, I couldn't get the name out of my mind.

I told many people this story and how perfect I thought that name would be in our family. My heart ached every time I talked about it. Each month, I secretly hoped Brandon's vasectomy would fail. I wanted another baby, but it seemed impossible.

*But the plans of the Lord stand firm forever, the purposes of his heart through all generations. -Psalm 33:11 NIV*

# Quicksand

*No one lights a lamp and then covers it with a bowl or hides it under a bed. A lamp is placed on a stand, where its light can be seen by all who enter the house. For all that is secret will eventually be brought into the open, and everything that is concealed will be brought to light and made known to all. -Luke 8:16-17 NLT*

Shortly before Lily was born, my marriage was in trouble, and I didn't realize it. After we got Logan to bed, Brandon would spend his evenings playing video games with his friends online while I sat on the computer on social media. Brandon played his game with a group of people that consisted of three or four guys and one girl. Lily's birth came and went. As we were adjusting to being a family of four, I noticed a lot of phone calls to one number which happened to be the girl of the group. Brandon swore it was nothing, but my suspicions grew.

One day, Brandon went out to run errands, and I was compelled to check his email. I had never done this before, but miraculously, I typed in the correct password. My heart sank as I read emails between him and this girl.

When Brandon came home, I confronted him. I had to restrain myself from throwing my cup of water at him. I had never been so mad or shocked in my life. I looked past him at a photo from our wedding, wondering where in the heck we went wrong. In that photo, we were looking into each other's eyes and smiling. We had so much love, excitement, and anticipation.

I called my friend, Courtney, who had been through something similar. She came right over. She and I went to the park with newborn Lily, and we talked for a long time.

Lily was very young, probably about four weeks old. Babies generally don't smile until six weeks, but Lily was smiling at me as if she were saying, "It's going to be okay, Mom." Our hearts were warmed by Lily's expressions, and we smiled back in amazement despite the horrible situation unfolding.

*Not only so, but we also rejoice in our sufferings, because we know that suffering produces perseverance; perseverance, character; and character, hope. -Romans 5:3-4 NIV*

After returning home from the park, Courtney watched the kids, so Brandon and I could go for a drive to talk. I honestly did not know what was going to happen. Oddly, instead of wanting to leave him, I was fiercely afraid he was going to leave me.

Once we got to the same park, we sat in silence for a while. I broke the silence and asked Brandon what he wanted. He said he didn't know what he wanted, and he just wanted to be by himself.

This brought me back to when we were in college. Brandon was going through a rough time with school, and he didn't know how to handle it. He said he wanted to be by himself, and he broke up with me. It was very sudden and difficult for me, but I had so much support from my parents, roommates and coworkers.

Exactly one week after the breakup, he called me at work and asked if we could talk that night. Of course, I agreed to meet him after my last class of the day. I sat restlessly in my psychology class that evening. The minutes seemed to drag on forever. Once class was dismissed, I ran to my car as fast as I could. Brandon was waiting for me with open arms, and we picked right back up where we left off. I really hoped this situation was going to end the same way but at the time, I didn't see how it was possible.

I felt like Brandon was going to break up with me again. But circumstances were much different this time. We were married, had children, a mortgage, car payment, and credit card debt. We could barely make ends meet, much less afford two separate households. Worst of all, I couldn't even fathom how difficult it would be to not see my children every day. I didn't know what to do. I didn't even think to pray, but God came to my rescue anyway and gave me the exact words I needed to say. The words seemed to come from thin air.

As I looked straight ahead at the open field, I said, "This is honestly the last thing I want to think about right now, but I am young, and I *will* move on. How will you feel when your kids have another dad, and I have another husband?"

It was like a flip of a switch, and he was snapped out of a trance. Without saying a word, Brandon took the extra flip phone he had bought to contact this person, got out of the car, put the phone under the back tire, got back in the driver's seat and drove over it back and forth. Then, he kissed me passionately and told me he was incredibly sorry.

We seemed like we were renewed somehow. For the next several nights, I would wake him up asking questions about what happened, and he would wake up instantly and patiently answer me. Then, comfort me until I fell back to sleep. He reassured me every chance he had that he was not going to do anything like that again. I felt just as confident as I did that morning after we met that he was not going anywhere.

*For the Holy Spirit will teach you at that time what you should say.*
*-Luke 12:12 NIV*

Things were good between Brandon and me for about a year. We were closer than we had ever been, but we slowly started falling into the same pattern. Him with the games and me with social media.

One night, I received a message from a guy I knew. I didn't think much of it. The thought or desire to cheat on Brandon never crossed my mind. But this guy and I started talking via messenger nearly daily. I found myself feeling giddy and teenage-like when hearing from him. Within a week, I told the guy we needed to stop talking, but he convinced me our talking was harmless.

Being a people-pleaser, I continued talking to him. I started to feel trapped. I was miserable unless I was talking to this person. It was like a drug addiction and each message was a hit of the drug. I noticed that each hour I went with no contact, I felt more like myself again, but the next message would send me all the way back. I started becoming a different person. Every responsibility I had in my life with work and my family was on the back burner.

After becoming incredibly miserable, I knew I had to do something. I told the guy once again I could not talk to him anymore. He didn't put up a fight that time. I blocked him from social media, phone, and email in case he changed his mind.

One night as we were eating dinner, I began to cry. Brandon demanded to know what was wrong. Maybe it crossed my mind to keep everything to myself, but I knew I had to tell him. If I didn't, the guilt would kill me, and I would feel like I was living a lie. Each time he'd showed me love; I would not fully accept it because I would know he was not loving the true me if he didn't know what happened.

I took him to our room and told him everything. He was so hurt. Suddenly, my feelings didn't matter to me. I was expecting him to ask for a divorce. He did the exact opposite. He told me he did not want to leave me, and he loved me. I realized in that moment that Brandon was demonstrating God's mercy and true love. I thought about how there are many people who go their entire lives on Earth searching for this kind of love, and they never find it.

*Above all, love each other deeply, because love covers a multitude of sins. -1 Peter 4:8 NIV*

Months later, another guy started flirting with me, and I was reminded of the same giddy feelings. I remember going to the drive-in movie with my family, which should have been an exciting and fun experience, yet I was feeling completely miserable.

I began to feel I was incapable of being the wife that Brandon deserved. I kept picturing myself sinking into mud, like quicksand. I sensed God pulling me out, but I kept sinking back in. It was over my head...suffocating me.

One night, I told Brandon I wanted to leave. Then, God provided the perfect words yet again. Brandon said, "I will get my vasectomy reversed."

At that moment, I realized my discontentment stemmed from wanting more children and regretting the vasectomy. Three years earlier, we chose not to listen to or even check with God when it came to our family planning, and our lives were nearly ruined because of it. Regardless, God saved our marriage time after time.

For the next several months, I listened to nothing but Christian music or pastors on satellite radio. This kept my mind in the right place as I drove alone in my car. The job I had at the time required a lot of travel during my workday.

I learned so much from those pastors. They taught me about scripture and how the devil is very real and seeks to destroy. Yet, God loves us and wants us to have a fulfilling life now, and for eternity. To make that possible, he sent his one and only son, Jesus to Earth. Jesus spent his time on Earth teaching, performing miracles, healing, and casting out demons. Jesus was the ultimate sacrifice and died on a cross so our sins could be forgiven. Jesus conquered the grave and rose from the dead. After spending more time on Earth, he ascended to Heaven. The wondrous life and work of Jesus is described in the gospel chapters of the bible: Matthew, Mark, Luke and John.

*"For God so loved the world that he gave his one and only Son, that whoever believes in him shall not perish but have eternal life. For God did not send his Son into the world to condemn the world, but to save the world through him." -John 3:16 NIV*

Even though I was learning from the bible and growing in my relationship with God more than ever before, there were still a few months of struggle. The devil tried his hardest to pull me back down. He'd throw ex-boyfriends in my path. I struggled with daydreaming. Love songs were a trigger for me.

One day, I went for a run. I was listening to my music on shuffle when a lullaby came on. I slowed down and eventually just stopped. God always seemed to use my kids to pull me out of the muddy quicksand and bring me back to reality.

I started crying right there at the entrance of a subdivision as I thought about Logan, Lily, and Brandon. I pictured the potential misery I could have caused for all of us. I prayed, apologizing to my heavenly father for following my own selfish ways, and I told Him I surrendered and was ready to follow Him. I dried my eyes, turned around, and ran back home. I didn't know it at the time, but a few years later, I realized this was the exact moment that God saved me from eternal misery.

*O Lord my God, I called to you for help and you healed me. O Lord, you brought me up from the grave; you spared me from going down into the pit. -Psalm 30:2-3 NIV*

From the moment I prayed that prayer of salvation, my life began to change. I experienced indescribable love, peace and joy for the first time. I noticed that certain things I did or did not do increased or decreased those feelings. I began to lose interest in prior pastimes. For example, Brandon and I used to watch scary movies, but I lost the desire to watch them.

I quit listening to love songs for a long time and listen to them sparingly even today. The difference is, when I hear a love song today, I'm reminded of Brandon. If a song comes on from that tragic time in my life and I'm reminded of someone other than Brandon, I quickly turn it off and thank God for freeing me from that misery.

As I began living a new life, I learned some strategies. Every time a guy contacts me, says something off, winks at me, or touches me, I tell Brandon as soon as possible. Before I started doing this, I would have thought about it and wondered why it happened and what it meant. It seems like when I bring it out in the light, it disappears from my mind.

Something else we do differently is give each other open access to our phones and email at all times. I have deleted my social media account many times but felt so isolated from the world as a result. I'm still trying to figure out a definitive solution but for now, Brandon and I have a joint social media account, and I strictly limit the amount of time I spend on it. Brandon and I have become accountability partners as all married couples should be. No marriage is bulletproof.

Years ago, I had a conversation with one of my coworkers who was about to retire. We were talking about her long marriage. I asked her about their success, and she made a comment that neither of them had been unfaithful to the other.

I was so envious of that at the time. Never in a million years did I think Brandon and I would go through what we did. But today, I am thankful for it in a way. Brandon and I are so close now. We work as a team and grow together. We have this unbelievable appreciation for each other that I doubt we would have if we hadn't nearly lost each other.

Life with Brandon is peaceful and easy on my heart. If we get mad at each other or don't see eye to eye, we apologize and forgive quickly and don't go to bed angry. God has taught us to love each other this way. He helped us so much, even before we took the time to get to know Him and follow His lead. Without God, I can't imagine where we would be today.

*"In your anger do not sin": Do not let the sun go down while you are still angry, and do not give the devil a foothold.*
*-Ephesians 4:26-27 NIV*

# Part 3:
# New Beginnings:
# Life His Way

# Reversing Our Mistake

*Therefore, since Christ suffered in his body, arm yourselves also with the same attitude, because he who has suffered in his body is done with sin. As a result, he does not live the rest of his earthly life for evil human desires, but rather for the will of God. -1 Peter 4:1-2 NIV*

Brandon kept his word on getting the vasectomy reversal. I had no idea how we were going to make it happen. The cost of a vasectomy reversal is daunting. It is typically over $10,000, but I found this doctor who took on a mission to reverse vasectomies at a fraction of the cost. This doctor had a similar story. He had a vasectomy himself, but he and his wife longed to have more children, so he had it reversed. They went on to have several more children after his reversal. His office was only about an hour and a half drive for us. We booked the earliest possible date in June 2013.

After a few weeks of anxiously waiting, the day had arrived. Brandon and I dropped the kids off at daycare and made our way to the familiar St. Louis area. I was so excited! When we arrived, I felt like we were at Disney World. Brandon was in great spirits, seemingly unphased by the procedure he was about to endure. Getting a vasectomy reversal was not much different than the vasectomy itself. It did take a lot longer, but Brandon did not seem to have discomfort or pain.

We left feeling renewed and excited about our new possibilities. We went out to eat at Brandon's favorite restaurant, The Spaghetti Factory. I felt like I was on cloud nine… a much purer and satisfying form of "giddy." I had no idea how badly I really wanted this, and I was sure God wanted it for us too.

Before the vasectomy and reversal, we had no issues conceiving. I typically got pregnant within two months of trying. I was sure it wouldn't take long to get pregnant after the reversal, but I was wrong. It took about one year. I was still healing and learning throughout that year. I think God was waiting until I was truly ready and committed to taking his lead before blessing us with our first vasectomy reversal baby.

On July 4, 2014, I went to Target with Logan and Lily to get a few items for the gathering we were having that night. I decided to get some pregnancy tests. I noticed the couple in front of us at the checkout had some tests as well. After having so many negative tests over the last year, I was sure that the couple's test would be positive and mine would be negative.

When we got home, the kids went off to play. Brandon was mowing the grass in the backyard. I decided to take the test. I saw one line right away thinking it was the control line. Then, I saw a fainter line pop up. I realized the first line that I saw was the test line. I was pregnant! I ran outside and asked Brandon to come inside because I had to show him something. We were both in disbelief as we looked at the very positive pregnancy test. That night, we had so much joy and excitement as we celebrated the Fourth of July with our family and watched the town's fireworks display from our driveway. To this day, the Fourth of July is one of our favorite holidays.

# Our Lucian

A few months after finding out I was pregnant, we had a gender reveal party. I went to a party store and gave them an envelop with the gender written on a piece of paper inside, so they would know whether to place blue or pink balloons in the wrapped box I provided. It was not easy, but I refrained from peeking as the box sat in our closet for about 24 hours.

Brandon and I invited our family and closest friends for the reveal, dinner and cake. We let Logan and Lily open the box as we stood by their side. Logan shouted, "They're blue!"

Lily was disappointed initially, but she eventually joined in the excitement. *Our* Lucian was finally joining our family. What once seemed so impossible in my mind was actually happening.

Life started really changing while I was pregnant with Lucian. At the time, I was a child abuse investigator, and it was a very demanding career. I was constantly on my laptop at home just to keep up. If I wasn't physically working, I was going over my to-do list in my head. I dreaded Monday morning chaos and extra work that had accumulated from the weekend. I couldn't go on vacation without working my tail off before I left and resuming the same pace when I returned. This was barely manageable with two young children. I couldn't imagine doing it with a newborn. So, I started looking for other positions within the agency that would be less demanding.

I came across a posting for a position at the 24-hour child abuse hotline. It had various shifts, including 4:00 PM-12:30 AM. I almost took this position months before I became pregnant but opted out because I knew it would be hard to see my kids since they went to school all day. But now that I was pregnant and had the opportunity again, I was beginning to see the advantages. I missed so much of Logan and Lily's younger years because of working demanding jobs with daytime hours. Working in the evening would allow me to take care of this baby all day. We would not have to pay for daycare. I could be there for Logan and Lily on days off school, Christmas vacation, spring break, and summers. I'd be there for them when they were home sick from school as well as before and after school. The kids would have me during the day and Brandon in the evening. What seemed like such a bad idea months before, now seemed like the best plan. I applied for the position, got the offer, and accepted it.

I started the new position with excitement. I felt so at peace with my decision. In fact, I can't think of a decision I've made in my life that I felt more at peace with. I completed my training and worked independently for two weeks before going into labor. This was just enough time for me to feel comfortable with the work and able to pick up where I left off when I returned from maternity leave.

One Monday night/early Tuesday morning after work, my coworkers and I were scraping ice off our windshields. I specifically remember one of my coworkers asking me a few times, "Are you sure you're okay? I can scrape your car for you."

I waved her off, assuring her I was fine. By this point, I was 38 weeks pregnant. I was ready to meet this baby. I had been walking up and down the stairs on my breaks. Scraping my car was another way to speed the process along. I drove home that night, parked in the garage, and had to sit in my car for a bit. I had a familiar pain. Earlier that day, the doctor I had seen informed me that the pain was contractions. Once the pain subsided enough, I went inside, did my bedtime routine of taking my vitamin, freshening up, and putting my pajamas on. Then, I dropped into bed next to Brandon.

I felt contractions seemingly nonstop all night long. Around 5:00 AM, I woke Brandon up in tears because of the pain I had tried to sleep through. We called the doctor's answering service, and they advised that I go to the hospital to get checked. I thought it was a false alarm until I noticed I had started bleeding.

When we got to the hospital, Brandon dropped me off at the front door, and he went to park the car. As soon as I walked through the door, I felt God's presence like a flood washing over me. My eyes filled with tears, and I broke down crying when I said I was there because I thought I was in labor. I was so excited to meet my little one, yet nervous about the c-section and a little sad that the pregnancy was coming to an end.

The resident doctor was really concerned about the bleeding. He was afraid I had placenta abruption, but that wasn't the case. I had not dilated at all, but I watched the monitor and noticed my contractions were a recognizable pattern. Each contraction created a little hill that was identical to the last. It was an amazing sight!

It was God's perfect timing because my doctor had been on vacation, but her first day back was the exact day I went into labor. She called the hospital and told me she knew that I was over being pregnant, and I was tired. She said that typically to have a c-section before 39 weeks, I had to have cervical change or dilation. However, since I was bleeding, she was confident we would be having a c-section that morning.

Shortly after the phone call, things started moving quickly. When they transferred me to another bed, I started shaking. I was crying from the pain of the contractions. The nurse looked at me sympathetically and said, "I've seen this over and over again. You may not be dilating, but I know you are in labor."

Lucian was born that morning and instantly filled our family with joy. To her grandmothers' dismay, Lily, age 5, would not share him at the hospital. She wanted to hold him all to herself.

We went from a family of four to a family of five. This was new territory for all of us. Logan and Lily were going to school at the time, so Lucian and I had a lot of time together. I felt like a first-time mom again. My days were filled with snuggles, walks, nursing and naps. I loved it! Having another baby in my life brought me indescribable joy.

*Now all glory to God, who is able, through his mighty power at work within us, to accomplish infinitely more than we might ask or think.*
*-Ephesians 3:20 NLT*

# Beginning Our Homeschool Journey

While I loved all the one-on-one time I had with Lucian, I felt very guilty about not seeing my older two children much at all since they were in school, and our schedules were opposite. It occurred to me that kids are in school a lot! As I sat at home missing them, I wondered what they could possibly be doing all day. It was very convenient when I was working days, but now that I was home all day, it didn't seem right to have them in school so much. Most moms have evenings to spend with their children and make up for lost time, but that wasn't the case for me since I worked later hours than the norm. Admittingly, I kept the kids home from school every now and then, just because we needed more time together.

Taking the kids out of school for a day here and there was not enough. The last thing I wanted was my kids looking back and thinking I was not there for them. Sadly, that was the path we were heading down. One night, the school had an open house. Logan's teacher excitedly showed us Logan's writing. He wrote something nice about Brandon and how he looks up to him because he fixes stuff. The part about me said I worked all the time and he rarely saw me. My heart broke. It took everything in me not to cry right there. It was my worst fear; my child saw me as a parent who was never around.

My heart ached every time I thought about this writing, and it still does. I longed to find a solution. I loved being home with Lucian all day, but I wanted to be with my other children more. God was about to make a suggestion.

In August 2015, we decided we needed to get a larger vehicle. I had a tiny Ford Fiesta, and it barely fit three kids in the backseat. So, we bought a Honda Odyssey minivan. We stayed at the dealership long after it had closed to finalize the sale.

We had to go in the next day to get the van detailed. I knew that it would likely take a long time, so I had the kids pack their backpacks with things to do. When we arrived, the car salesman asked if my kids were homeschooled. My response was, "Heck no!"

The idea to homeschool hadn't occurred to me. I never considered it an option for my children's education. The car salesman explained that his wife homeschooled their children. He told me about a program they used. He said that she would send in all their papers and tests for grading. I firmly believe this information was a seed planted by God at just the right time. As we were getting ready to embark on another school year, I was intrigued. We had so much fun over the summer, and I loved being with my kids all day long. I was dreading sending them back to school.

About a week later, Lily was at gymnastics. As I was watching her from the parent viewing area, I noticed a couple of kids next to me working on workbooks. I asked their grandmother, who was helping them if they were by chance homeschooled. The grandmother said they were. Then, she directed me to their mother who had a wealth of information about homeschooling in our area. She told me all about the groups available such as co-ops and YMCA Homeschool PE. She advised that curriculum can be purchased at a reasonable price. She showed me the books she was using for her young children that she had purchased from Barnes & Noble.

I was surprised to hear she had been a teacher herself at the same public school my children were attending, yet she felt that homeschooling was the best way to educate her children. She talked about how homeschooling only takes a few hours a day. I was shocked by this. I said, "I sit at home all day missing my kids who are in school from 8:00 AM to 2:00 PM, which is six hours. We can spend half the amount of time and get the same result?"

The teacher explained to me that in school, a lot of time is spent with transitions and helping kids who are further behind or having behavioral issues. She assured me that it is indeed possible to get it all done in a fraction of the time. The idea of homeschooling was very new to me, but a week after the seed was planted, I was sold. I just had to get up the nerve to mention the seemingly crazy idea to Brandon.

One night at work, while I was pumping milk for Lucian, I couldn't wait any longer to tell Brandon what had been on my heart for the last couple of weeks. I had no idea how he would react. We had never considered homeschooling or even brought it up in conversation. We both went to public school and hadn't considered other options.

I called him and said, "Don't think I'm crazy, but how would you feel about me homeschooling Logan and Lily?"

He had a similar response that I did when I was first introduced to the idea. He pointed out that I was already stretched thin with working full-time, not getting much sleep, and having three kids. Plus, it was just so out of the norm. In any case, the seed had been planted in his mind, God worked on his heart, and he eventually came around to the idea.

As Brandon and I discussed the possibility of homeschooling, we looked back on the education our kids had up to that point. Lily did one year of kindergarten in a private school because she missed the age requirement at the public school by three days, and we felt she was ready for kindergarten. She did a second year of kindergarten in public school but could have done first grade instead. However, we were not aware this was an option until after the fact.

Logan completed two years of kindergarten in public school because he had a late birthday and wasn't ready to move on after the first year. He was in second grade when we began to consider homeschooling. Second grade was difficult for Logan. He would say the days seemed long, and it wasn't as fun as kindergarten and first grade. He noticed his teacher favored the girls over the boys. He was ahead of the other kids in math but was forced to do work that was too easy for him.

Logan reports that even when he went to school, he learned more from home. He learned multiplication from Brandon before they started learning it in school. He says he learned how to read from me. I don't remember actively teaching him how to read, but coincidentally, it happened. Logan, Lily, and I would often sit in their rooms and do flashcards and read books together while curled up with blankets, laughing, and enjoying each other's company.

Logan has a vivid memory of me teaching him about long vowels and silent E's as we were waiting to get our food at a restaurant. He was so proud of himself! Oddly, his teacher confused him as he tested his new skill at school. He ran up to her and asked her how to spell "time." She told him T-I-M. He went back to his seat, puzzled. Maybe there is some sort of kindergarten teacher logic to misinforming him, but part of me wonders if she was keeping him from getting too far ahead of his peers.

I was very tempted to pull our kids out of school after Christmas vacation but didn't. As the kids finished out the school year, I spent time praying, researching, and planning. I was so excited and interested in the topic of homeschooling and curriculum. On the last day of school, I decorated the kitchen with signs that said things like "Welcome Summer!" I was so excited to launch this new lifestyle. I was relieved knowing I would not have to hand my kids over after spending the summer together.

*These commandments that I give you today are to be upon your hearts. Impress them on your children. Talk about them when you sit at home and when you walk along the road, when you lie down and when you get up. -Deuteronomy 6:6-9 NIV*

# *Leland*

After I had Lucian, I knew I was not done having kids. It felt off having an odd number of children. Plus, Logan and Lily were so much older than Lucian. I felt that Lucian needed a sibling closer to his age. We still had all of Lucian's baby stuff, and it didn't seem right to use it for one baby for a short amount of time. I prayed about it, and to my surprise, Brandon was on board. I was nervous about what other people would say if we had a fourth child, but I knew God put that desire in my heart, and if it was His will, it would happen.

Leland joined our family about two years after Lucian. I got pregnant with him right away. I felt nauseous all day long for several months. I looked forward to sleeping because that was the only time that I felt relief. It was a struggle to continue working but I managed somehow. It took every ounce of energy to walk from the parking lot to my desk. I napped in my car on my 15-minute breaks. On my meal breaks, I roamed the grocery store trying to find something that sounded remotely appealing. I searched my phone for ideas on how women handled difficult pregnancies. I don't think I found a solution, but I was comforted knowing I wasn't alone.

About a week before Leland's scheduled c-section, I started feeling like I was going into labor, so Brandon and I went to the hospital just in case. I was having contractions but not dilating. They had me walk the halls some. Brandon and I were cheerful and enjoyed the stroll together. They ended up sending me home that night. Leland must have been comfortable in my belly because he did not come out until he was forced to on his scheduled c-section at the end of March.

The feelings I had after Leland's birth were similar to that of Lily's. I had more confidence. He took up nursing very well and just seemed to be a content baby…as long as he was being held, of course. Brandon and the kids were able to visit us every day. We had a family photo taken hours after Leland was born. Little did I know, that was the last birth that my other children would visit me at the hospital. Logan and Lily loved visiting. Logan loved the pizza in the cafeteria. Lily loved the cookies. I enjoyed being able to see them as I was healing, bonding with the new baby and preparing to go home.

Leland was a happy baby with a vibrant personality. When he was about six months old, we went on a vacation at Wisconsin Dells. We roamed the winding halls, exploring the resort on our first night. Logan was talking to Leland and kept raising his arms as he talked. Leland thought it was the funniest thing ever and would laugh this big belly laugh over and over again. It brought a smile and even chuckles to people we passed by in the halls. He lit up the entire place with his little baby laugh. It didn't stop there. Leland loves to laugh. He finds reasons to laugh every day, and it still brings a smile to my face every time. I love the laughter of all my children, but his laugh is uniquely endearing.

Leland may have an excellent sense of humor, but he is also very strong-willed. He must do everything on his own terms. Although it requires a little extra work on our part, I'm glad Leland is strong-willed. I know he is going to be very successful one day. When he is out of sorts, he is usually calmed with an activity that makes him think, like a puzzle or a book. He really likes to use his mind. He is motivated and has an excellent attention span.

Leland is an anxious child. He often tells me what he's worried about, and I encourage him to do so. Some of his fears are floods, fires, getting eaten by various animals, and falling through a hole or crack in the ground. It is heartbreaking yet interesting to hear what Leland worries about. I imagine they are common concerns for children.

*When anxiety was great within me, your consolation brought joy to my soul. -Psalm 94:19 NIV*

# *Landry*

Throughout my entire pregnancy with Leland, I said he was my last one, but I felt a little tug every time I said it. As my doctor was performing my fourth c-section, she said, "Wow, you look great, very little scar tissue."

She was absolutely amazed by the condition of my uterus and even said we could have more children if we wanted. Brandon and I both exclaimed, "No!" but I knew right then and there that God was not done blessing us with children.

Shortly after Leland's first birthday, I had symptoms that suggested I was pregnant again. I worried about how we would handle five children. As Brandon and I watched a movie one night, I looked at our mantle lined with photos of our children, noting there was no more room for a fifth frame. I began to cry and told Brandon I thought I was pregnant. He comforted me and assured me it was going to be okay, and we would make it work. He even said it may be nice to have more because he was enjoying having all the kids. I immediately went to the grocery store and picked up a pregnancy test. It was negative.

I began to feel a void. I realized I wanted that test to be positive after my discussion with Brandon. One day, I sheepishly told him I didn't feel done having babies, and he agreed he wanted to have another. Once again, I was elated yet filled with fear about what others would think about us. Yet, I felt that the Lord was satisfied with our decision. It wasn't long before I was pregnant with Landry.

Landry's birthday was memorable. I was very excited about our c-section that was scheduled on a late-February morning. I was filled with anticipation and barely slept the entire night before. Then, around 5:00 AM, Lily came into our room crying. She was burning hot, had a high fever, and said she had a headache. After being a mom for over 10 years, I knew what those symptoms meant, especially in February. She had the flu.

My parents, Brandon, and I had a huddle before we left for the hospital. I arranged for my mom to take Lily to Prompt Care and get a prescription for herself and my dad for Tamiflu if Lily did, in fact, have the flu.

Brandon and I joined hands and prayed once we arrived at the hospital. We prayed that Lily's flu test would be negative, but if it wasn't, Lily and everyone in the family would be okay. Minutes before I went into the operating room, my mom called with the flu test results...positive.

I tried not to worry about the news I had just received as they were delivering my fifth child, but I was disheartened. Few things stress me out more than having a sick child, especially if it is an illness that can be easily passed to the others. I thought, "I don't care what the doctor says this time about me not having scar tissue. I'm done having babies."

My hands were beyond full already, and here I was bringing another baby into the family. Just as these thoughts were swarming around in my head, I heard not only the doctor but several nurses and other people in the room say, "Wow, it's like you've never had a c-section."

"It's amazing!"

"I've never seen anything like it."

"They were just meant to have a large family, born this way."

Holding Landry for the first time made my worries disappear. I showered him with kisses. I knew I shouldn't have because I may have had the flu too or at least the germs, but I couldn't resist. He was sweet as can be. However, the feelings of elation quickly changed back to worry as I got news about the situation at home. One by one, my kids were falling ill with the flu. They all had fevers, headaches and no energy. I felt helpless. I wanted to be there for my sick kids and take care of them, but at the same time, I wanted to stay far away to protect Landry. Little did I know, I should have been protecting Landry from myself.

Around midnight on Landry's first night, I started getting the chills. My temperature was going up but not too high because they had me on all sorts of pain medication that incidentally reduces fevers. The next morning, my doctor talked me into getting a flu test, and it was, you guessed it...positive.

After receiving a positive influenza result, everyone who entered my room had a mask on. I wore a mask as well. There were caution signs on my door. I was not allowed to leave the room. I was so afraid that they would take Landry from me, but they did the opposite. They kept him in my room the entire time. They did not take him out to weigh him but brought the scale to us.

The pediatrician visited us in our room each morning to check Landry over. We discussed the other kids and how they were doing at home. I told her about how well Brandon was taking care of them. He'd line them all up to take their temperatures and give them their medicine. The pediatrician showed me more support than anyone at the hospital. She did not act worried about catching the flu, maybe because she was around sick kids all day anyway. She held Landry a little longer one morning so I could eat breakfast. This was heartwarming because all the nurses and hospital staff would hurry out of my room after completing whatever task they came in for.

My mom and dad were also supportive. They were my main visitors since Brandon was needed at home. We spent the days watching movies and passing Landry around. I was so happy to have them with me, but I felt homesick. I wanted Brandon. I thought it was interesting. As a child, when I was sick, I wanted my mom and dad. As an adult, I want my husband. I often thought about this even before Landry's birth and conversed with friends about it. Growing up, I had feelings of comfort, peace, and joy from my dad. Now that I'm married to Brandon, I get comfort from him. That gives me confidence that I'm married to the right man. I hope more than anything that my children feel the same way in their marriages one day.

*For this reason, a man will leave his father and mother and be united to his wife, and they will become one flesh. -Genesis 2:24 NIV*

We all made it through the flu. Brandon, Landry, and my parents were spared from the virus. Landry was a good baby. He has always been a bit calmer. He loves to find a cozy spot and lie down with a book or toy. He seems to enjoy quiet time at bedtime, alone in his bed. He nearly always has a smile on his face. He absolutely loves getting visitors at our home. He isn't shy or bothered by new people. Before he could talk, he would reach his arms up to be held by anyone who entered our home. Once he turned two, his speech really took off, and he started talking to visitors. He is a true blessing!

Having five children was a major adjustment for me. I often hear parents say they noticed a difference going from two to three children. I say adding one more child, no matter how many you have, is an adjustment. If I had to choose, adding a fifth. was my most difficult adaptation. Logan and Lily were well-behaved and helpful. However, Lucian was struggling with a speech delay. Strong-willed Leland was in his terrible twos. Landry was a good baby, but he was still a newborn requiring a lot of care and attention.

One day at our homeschool co-op, Leland melted down when it was time to go home. Landry was freaking out because he wanted to eat. Even with my parents' help, we were still putting on quite a show for the other homeschool moms. I desperately wanted everyone to think I had it all together and could handle five kids just fine. I thought that if I didn't seem to have things under control, they would think that is why people should not have so many children. On this particular day, it was apparent that I did NOT have it all together. By the time my dad and I got the kids to the car, I was in tears. My dad wrapped his arm around me and assured me it would get easier.

My dad was right. Things did get easier after a few months as we got into a routine of being a family of seven. One day as I watched my children run around in our backyard, I decided to see if it was possible for us to get a larger home. The idea seemed to come out of nowhere. Our income had just increased significantly, so I figured it wouldn't hurt to try. I called our lender we had used for previous home purchases and set up a time to meet with her.

That weekend, Brandon and I started looking at homes with a realtor. We found a home we loved and got pre-approval from our lender the next day. Just as we were getting ready to meet with our realtor to submit an offer, the house sold. We were crushed and completely heartbroken. However, within a few days, we found a better home. We learned that we had to sell our house before putting in an offer for a new one. Our house was on the market for less than 24 hours and sold on the Fourth of July…another reason why we love that holiday.

We took Logan, Lily, and baby Landry to see the house we had picked out. Then, we went to see a few other homes just to be sure we were choosing the best fit. That evening, we put in an offer, and it was accepted.

After we had contracts secured, it was time for inspections and repairs. The home we were selling was new but had some issues, including a major leak. Money seemingly popped up just when we needed it, as did repair men.

As our closing day approached, I learned that the house we initially wanted went back on the market. After getting that bit of information, Brandon and I realized without a doubt that God guided us to the best home for our family. I also think God gave me a nudge to start the process at just the right time. If we had waited six months longer, we would have been doing it all in the middle of the COVID-19 pandemic when the price of homes increased drastically.

Our new home makes a world of difference. The kids all had their own rooms at one point, but Leland and Lucian decided they want to share a room. That gave us an extra room to make a sitting area for me to study, read and write. We also have Logan and Lily's desks in that room so they can do their schoolwork with me close by. The basement and three-car garage both come in handy when it's too cold or rainy to play outside. The yard is fenced in, so we no longer have to chase after escaping toddlers.

Brandon and I often look around our home just in awe of how God not only saved us and our marriage but how much He blessed us and how far He had taken us from where we once were.

*And God will generously provide all you need. Then you will always have everything you need and plenty left over to share with others. -2 Corinthians 9:8 NLT*

# Bump in the Road:
# ASD Diagnosis

Lucian was a serious baby, but he did smile and hit most of his milestones. He was walking by nine months. I started to worry when he was 18 months and not speaking at all. I wasn't overly concerned because Logan did not say much at that age either. However, the pediatrician suggested that early intervention become involved.

Leland came along shortly after Lucian started early intervention, and I would have to discretely nurse Leland on the couch while the speech therapist worked with Lucian on our living room floor. One of Lucian's speech therapists mentioned that Lucian seemed to have some sensory stuff going on. He would lie down and look at the car wheels when he played with cars. He seemed to like to be squeezed or have pressure on his arms, legs, and head. Brandon and I also noticed that Lucian seemed to have a very high pain tolerance. For example, he would put very hot food in his mouth and not seem to notice it was hot. He would get a bump on his head or cut on his finger and barely cry. We also became aware that Lucian would stiffen up in response to any nurturing touch commonly exchanged between parents and their children, such as putting our hand on his shoulder or trying to hold his hand. It wasn't a stiffness of defiance. It was a signal that he was not comfortable and did not like the gestures. Several therapists hinted Lucian might have autism, but I was in complete denial until I had no choice but to come to terms with it in March 2019, shortly after Landry was born.

Lucian had an evaluation with a child psychologist and developmental pediatrician. I nervously sat in the room with Lucian and the doctors. I was already in a fragile state, having just given birth to Landry a few weeks before. I was emotional and afraid to know. The doctor told me that whatever the outcome of the assessment, I would be walking out with the same kid I came in with. Somehow, this was not at all comforting to me. Yes, it would be the same kid, and I love him dearly, but the diagnosis would leave me with so many questions that they would be unable to answer. Would it get worse? Will he live with Brandon and me forever? Will he ever get married?

Will he talk or communicate effectively? Is it okay to homeschool him like his siblings?

Lucian showed the doctors everything they needed to see during the assessment. He did random repetitive behaviors like roll cars or place toys on his belly. He kept taking an object out of his pocket and pretending to eat something from it. This was a behavior I rarely saw before, but he must have done it ten times in the thirty minutes we were in the assessment. He did not engage much unless it was exciting, like pretending to have a birthday party. By the end of the assessment, with my bachelor's degree in psychology (minor in special education) and all the research I had done online, I knew what the doctors were going to tell me. That did not keep the tears from rolling down my cheeks when I heard it out loud, "Lucian has ASD (Autism Spectrum Disorder)."

After seeing my tears, Lucian immediately got up from playing, came right to me, and gave me a hug. The doctors were astonished and said, "We don't see children do that in here."

Still in denial, I thought, "That's because he does not have autism."

I received the written evaluation in the mail, and it clearly stated in the recommendations that Lucian should go to pre-k instead of homeschooling. Knowing it was not God's plan or what I wanted to do, I sent Lucian to pre-k. It went well for a couple of months. Lucian seemed to love going to school. My other kids had more of my attention since Lucian often takes a lot of my attention. But we all missed him. Our family dynamics were not the same without him.

By October, Lucian no longer willingly went to school. At one point, teachers had to nearly drag him in. His speech was not improving, and if anything, it was getting worse. To top it off, he was bringing illnesses home and sharing germs with his siblings.

*Therefore, dear friends, since you already know this, be on your guard so that you may not be carried away by the error of lawless men and fall from your secure position. -2 Peter 3:17 NIV*

We took a short trip to Arkansas that November to see Brandon's sister get married. It was so nice having all the kids together and not having to worry about sending Lucian to school those few days. By the end of the trip, Lucian was getting back to his normal self, and our family felt whole again. Brandon and I decided to pull Lucian from pre-k, and he did not return to school.

Within a week of being out of school, Lucian was less anxious and talking more. We had given school a try, but it wasn't for him. I realized I know my child and what is best for him much better than a psychologist who spent less than an hour with him. God knew all along but patiently waited for me to see it for myself.

We have come to terms that Lucian is different, and while he may have autism, it is very mild. His main issue continues to be speech and attention. Lucian still stiffens up, but he does show affection. Sometimes, he'll stop me and give me a kiss on my hand or ask for a hug. His speech is still delayed but improving. He is not obsessed with cars like he used to be, but he has moved on to Mario and Sonic. He has only played video games a handful of times, but talks about Mario and Sonic often. When I tell him to talk about something besides Mario and Sonic, he talks about Jesus. He loves bible stories!

Aside from some attention issues, Lucian learns pretty well. He does best one-on-one in a room without distractions. He will listen to book after book. It turns out that homeschooling is perfect for him because we can move at a pace that is best for him. We don't take summers off to keep up the momentum. I know his cues that say it is time to take a break. If something isn't working well, I can make changes to our curriculum.

The interesting thing about Lucian is that he can be very engaging and seemingly neurotypical at times. Then, he hits these regressions. He withdraws and obsesses over certain things. There have been times when all he would do was look at his Mario sticker book for days. Then, it occurred to us to take the sticker book away and limit time with it just like we limit screen time. Within a day, Lucian would start engaging with us more and play with his siblings again.

Brandon and I are constantly observing him and setting limits for him. Lucian is learning to set his own limits as a result. Now, there are times that Lucian brings us a certain toy and tells us he needs a break from it. I didn't get the idea to set limits from a book or the internet. Brandon and I are not experts on autism, but we are experts on our children.

# Working From Home

After Landry was born, I was still working evenings at the child abuse hotline. I had moved into a temporary supervisory role. The work was quite different and stressful at times.

In December 2019, I attended a supervisor meeting/Christmas gathering. We were told that they were considering allowing workers to work from home, but it was going to be a long process. To start, we were going to do a trial with only a few workers. I was discouraged to hear supervisors would have to continue working in the office.

As I sat in the meeting, my mind began to wander thinking about all the good things that would result from working from home. With no late-night commute, I would get to bed thirty minutes earlier. I could have the lighting and temperature in my workspace to my liking. I could go on evening walks or bike rides with my family during my breaks.

I have wanted to work from home since I became a mother. I recalled being envious of Courtney when she was working from home while her children were young. One evening, we were hanging out with our kids having a good time. My enjoyment was hindered knowing I would have to leave my children the following morning so I could go to work. I told Courtney how nice it must have been for her to not ever have to leave her children when she worked. She humbly agreed it was really nice. Working evenings was much better for me since I was with my children a lot more during the day, but I still missed them terribly while I was away.

The opportunity to work from home seemed too good to be true, and I doubted it would happen anytime soon, but I prayed about it anyway. I asked on the way home, "Oh Lord, could it be possible?"

I firmly believe that God likes specific prayers, so I asked that within one year, I'd be working from home in the supervisor role, despite them saying supervisors would not be working from home.

Around the time of the Christmas meeting, there was talk about a virus that originated in China and was making its way to America…the coronavirus or COVID-19. Brandon was concerned, but I wasn't. He told me that it could be really bad, but I figured there had been other viruses like this that were contained, and I did not think this would be any different.

Against his advice, which I should never do, I booked our summer vacation to Long Beach, California. We wouldn't normally travel that far or lavishly, but Lily had a gymnastics meet scheduled there in June.

*Wives, submit to your husbands as to the Lord. -Ephesians 5:22* NIV

In March 2020, things started spiraling quickly. The governor abruptly closed schools. Grocery stores were swarmed with people. The shelves were bare. The hot commodities were cleaning supplies, bottled water, and toilet paper. People were in absolute panic. Surprisingly, as I strolled through Meijer to get a few items we needed, I felt a sense of peace. God was with us all and would see us through one way or another. I thought it was sad that most of the people in the store that day did not have that kind of peace.

*And the peace of God, which transcends all understanding, will guard your hearts and minds in Christ Jesus. -Philippians 4:7 NIV*

Coronavirus was new, and professionals did not know much about it. Some people who got it would have no symptoms. However, it was leaving others gravely ill, requiring hospitalization and intubation. Tragically, it was also killing people. The scary part was nobody knew how it would affect them or their family. You could be one of the lucky ones with no symptoms, or you could lose your life from it. This was the reason for the panic. All we could do was play it safe and stay home, away from others. People only left their homes for imperative reasons such as grocery shopping. Everyone was expected to wear face masks when they did go out.

Before coronavirus, I would see a random person or two with masks on and wonder why they were wearing masks. Were they trying to keep themselves from getting sick? Or protecting others from catching what they had? However, by Spring 2020, it was unusual to see anybody without a mask.

As COVID-19 was unfolding, we had another supervisor meeting that was very impromptu. We were informed that within one week, we would all be working from home, even supervisors. I was in complete disbelief. Just a couple of months before, working from home seemed too good to be true, but it was happening. I had faith that God was going to answer my specific prayer but never imagined it would happen so quickly. It all seemed surreal to me. Like everything was moving full speed with no sound, perhaps like being back on the Zipper with Annie.

Two years later, I am still working from home. I have a slightly different schedule, 2:00 PM to 10:30 PM, Monday through Friday. There is no plan to return to the office aside from a day or two a month. Working at home is everything I hoped it would be. When I worked at the office, I only saw Brandon for thirty minutes a day. I see him a lot more now. Instead of eating dinner alone in my car, I have dinner with my family. After dinner, I often go for a walk in the comfort of my own subdivision. Over the years, I missed so many nights of tucking my little ones in but now I get to give goodnight hugs and say bedtime prayers nightly. At the office, later in my shift, I missed my kids even knowing they were all sleeping. Now, when the kids are all in bed, I enjoy peace and quiet, knowing they are sleeping safely under the same roof as me. It is everything I had been wanting for over a decade. I feel like I am getting back "double portion" of the lost time with my family.

*Instead of shame and dishonor, you will enjoy a double share of honor. You will possess a double portion of prosperity in your land, and everlasting joy will be yours. -Isaiah 61:7 NLT*

# Layla

*For God does speak- now one way, now another- though man may not perceive it. In a dream, in a vision of the night, when deep sleep falls on men as they slumber in their beds, -Job 33:14-15 NIV*

Before our fifth child, Landry was born, Brandon said it was time to be done having children. I had said the entire pregnancy I was ready to be done as well. One day, I was in the kitchen having one of many struggles with my toddler (Leland) as I waddled around, very pregnant with Landry. I thought, "This is it. I have finally reached my limit. No more kids for me."

Shortly after Landry was born, I got the copper IUD. However, deep down, I really did not think I was done having kids. I pushed the feeling aside and I started to come to terms with Landry being our last. I started picturing our lives moving forward without adding another baby. I could focus more on homeschooling. We could go on more vacations. I could write this book. Then, I started getting some unwanted side effects from the IUD and ultimately decided to have it removed. We used temporary birth control until I got up the courage to have my tubes tied.

One night, I had this dream that I will never forget. I was pregnant and went to my doctor. She waved an ultrasound wand over my stomach. She enlarged a circle on the screen displaying the most beautiful baby girl I had ever seen with dark hair, big blue eyes and rosy cheeks. The baby was wearing an outfit that was the purest white with butterflies all over it.

To me, this dream seemed to be from God. My first clue was the pure white. Second, the butterflies. Years ago, I read a devotional that advised coming up with a sign between me and God, and "butterflies" instantly came to mind. With my stifled yearning for more children and this dream, I was almost certain that God wanted us to have another baby. I could not get that beautiful baby out of my mind. I tearfully told Brandon about the dream. I was shocked when his response was, "Let's have one more."

About two months later, I saw that familiar positive on a pregnancy test. As I was pregnant with baby number six, I truly felt complete. My doctor was very supportive of each pregnancy, but I sensed she was getting a little worried about me having so many c-sections. I was 38 years old, and my body was starting to feel tired of being pregnant. I also had debilitating migraines and couldn't really take any medication to help.

I talked to God throughout the pregnancy about my wishes to have my tubes tied during the c-section. I was at peace with the decision and did not have the turmoil and reservations that I had when it came to birth control after all my other children. I felt that God was ready to give me some new assignments that did not involve having more babies, at least not biologically.

On September 24, 2020, Brandon and I were out to dinner for our 15th wedding anniversary. I was excited because our next stop was at an ultrasound studio to find out if we were having a boy or girl. Deep down, I already knew the gender. During dinner conversation, I suggested that we go to the consignment store across the street and buy one girl outfit and one boy outfit and put the correct one in a gift bag with little gifts for all the kids. Then, without thinking consciously, I said, "We can just put the boy outfit in storage with the rest of the boy stuff we won't need anymore."

I gasped right after I said that and could not believe how sure my subconscious was that we were finally having a second baby girl. The ultrasound confirmed it. The baby's older siblings were ecstatic when they found out the news. Lily sobbed tears of happiness. She was finally getting a sister! Leland slept with the ultrasound pictures. We added "Layla" to our bedtime prayers from that night on.

My scheduled c-section with Layla was on a Monday. I started my maternity leave the Thursday before to get ready for her and spend time with the rest of the family. By Saturday, Brandon and I were doing everything we could to stay busy. That evening, we were tired. Brandon really did not want to clean the bathrooms which was the last thing on our to-do list. He said it could wait until the next day. However, I insisted on cleaning them that night.

After cleaning the bathrooms and getting all the kids to bed, Brandon and I watched one of our favorite TV shows. In the episode we watched, the women happened to be talking about the 4-1-1 rule. It's time to go to the hospital if you have four contractions lasting at least one minute for one hour.

We went to bed at about 11:00 PM that night. I kept tossing and turning and could not get comfortable. I got aggravated because as soon as I finally fell asleep, Brandon's snoring woke me up. I moved to the couch around midnight.

Around 2:00 AM, I woke up for about the fifth or sixth time, noticing that every time I woke up, my back was hurting. I realized I was having contractions. I thought about the 4-1-1 rule and decided to time the contractions. For one hour, I had contractions exactly four minutes apart and each contraction lasted one minute. I started to get excited. *Could we be having our baby girl one day early?* Then, I remembered I never dilate, and I was sure it was false labor. I had been lying down for all those contractions, and I figured they would stop when I stood up and walked around. I went to the bathroom, and they seemed to slow down, so I went back to sleep around 4:00 AM.

Logan came up from his room before 6:00 AM. I felt different. This time, I felt crampy in my belly as well as my back. I told him I thought I was in labor but wasn't sure. He turned the fan on for me because I was hot and then turned it off again when I said it was too cold. Logan is very sweet and has such a serving heart. He wanted to do all he could for me, but I told him to go ahead and go back downstairs to his room to rest. I turned the TV on for distraction. I still thought it was false labor. I planned to eat breakfast and have Brandon drop me off at the hospital, so they could confirm it was false labor and advise me to come back the following day.

After Brandon woke up and realized what was happening, he talked me out of eating anything, and I am glad he did. I went up and took a shower. As I was getting out of the shower, I lost some yellow fluid. I immediately thought it was amniotic fluid, and it had meconium in it. I hollered for Brandon to call my mom and have her and my dad come watch the kids so he could take me to the hospital.

I quickly got dressed, pausing between contractions. My mind was a blur as I tried to make sure I had everything packed for the hospital. We made our way downstairs and were about ready to get into the car when I felt another gush of fluid. By this time, I was pretty sure I was having Layla in a matter of hours, but still, in the back of my mind, I thought the labor would stop.

On the drive to the hospital, I noticed my contractions were two minutes apart. They were painful enough for me to stop talking and grab hold of the door handle. When Brandon and I arrived at the hospital, we were a little nervous. This hospital was new to us. I wasn't permitted to have a tubal ligation at the hospital we normally went to for our births as it was a Catholic hospital. It was a tough decision, but we reluctantly went to the hospital down the road from our normal one.

Once we entered the hospital, there was a familiar line of people waiting to get their temperatures taken and answer COVID questions. The lady in front of us asked, "Are you having a baby?"

Brandon said, "Yes."

She said, "You guys go ahead in front of me. I know every minute counts!"

We thanked her and moved up. I laid my head on Brandon as I got another contraction.

We passed the temperature checks. I told the attendant that I thought I was in labor. Forgoing the routine COVID questions, she said, "Oh my…you guys go on up to the 7th floor."

I was sure the contractions were going to slow down or change at any point, but they didn't as we made our way up the elevator and waited at the check-in desk. A new employee was learning how to check people in. I tried to be patient, bracing myself on the counter with each contraction.

Once we were checked in, our nurse walked us to our room. She had been observing me and decided it was likely real labor. She said, "You are in a lot of pain. I bet you are having this baby today."

A second nurse gave me a gown to change into. My mind was so fuzzy. I could barely think enough to do this task. When I climbed into the bed, I felt a much larger gush of fluid. I tried not to get my hopes up but was certain it was amniotic fluid. Still in disbelief, I knew they were going to check to see if I had dilated yet. I was sure I hadn't.

There was a very kind hospitalist who came into my room. He was older and quiet. When he checked me, I braced myself because it was usually very painful. This time, it wasn't too painful. He said I was one centimeter dilated, which shocked me. In all my previous births, I had never dilated at all. However, with my contractions being so close, I probably should have been near the pushing stage by this point. He also did a test to see if my water had indeed broken, and then he left the room. The nurse said the test takes up to 20 minutes but was already showing positive. My water had broken, and we were having the baby! I was so excited! Wow, the moment I had been waiting eagerly for the last several months was finally here. We were going to meet our baby girl!

Once they determined my water had broken, it was a whirlwind. Hospital staff kept coming in and out of the room. They started an IV and gave me medicine. Brandon was texting our families with updates. I continued to have contractions that forced me to grab onto the bedrails and push myself up off the bed. Brandon looked concerned and as if he felt helpless. Although this was our sixth delivery, intense labor was new to both of us. The nurse who did not leave my side the entire time, told him the contractions were two minutes apart, and I was handling them well. I looked at the monitor and saw the familiar hills that each contraction made just like before I had Lucian. We were sure to capture a picture this time.

The on-call doctor came in to speak with us. The doctor seemed to be discouraged since it was my sixth c-section. I needed this doctor to go into this with a positive attitude. Instead, she talked to us about how the risks go up with each c-section. She told us it was possible I had so much scar tissue that she may need to do a larger incision up and down my abdomen instead of a bikini incision. She also said that she might not be able to get to my fallopian tubes because of scar tissue. My doctor had discussed risks with me but never mentioned having to do an abdominal incision or not being able to get to my fallopian tubes. Brandon and I felt very uneasy by the time the on-call doctor left the room.

The time came to wheel me back to the operating room. This is my least favorite part about having babies. They separate me from Brandon which makes me cry every time. Brandon is my biggest source of support in life. So, it is difficult to go through a spinal and get prepped for surgery without him. As the anesthesiologist completed the spinal, a nurse stood in front of me, holding me still as tears of fear silently streamed down my face. I was so worn out from all the contractions that my head fell involuntarily on this stranger's shoulder.

After my anesthesia was in place, they quickly laid me down and started the prep work. I looked around the room in search of a little window so I could see a reflection like I could at the hospital where my other births had taken place. This was my way of sneaking a peak at what was behind the drape in front of my face. I spotted a window on a door that went to a small room where the doctor was standing, getting ready to come in. I noted she still looked like she had a bad attitude.

After what seemed to be an eternity, Brandon was at my side, and the familiar procedure commenced. We waited quietly for our little one to enter the world. I worried about Layla nearly the entire pregnancy, taking note of her every move or lack of movement because her umbilical cord had two vessels instead of three. I wondered how it was possible to have a perfectly normal baby with a two-vessel cord when it was supposed to have three vessels. We had extra ultrasounds to confirm she was okay, but I was worried most of the pregnancy.

I heard the doctor say that my doctor was correct; I healed unbelievably well. The hospitalist concurred. The doctor seemed to relax, and so did I. Then, I heard something about fingernails, and the baby was green because there was meconium in the amniotic fluid. I started to worry about aspiration but was relieved by Layla's first cries. She was here, and she was safe and healthy!

It seemed like they kept her away longer than my others. I kept asking Brandon if she was okay. I didn't hear her crying much. He kept looking over at her and then back at me, reassuring me she was fine, just "super chill." Eventually, he was able to bring her over to me. As always, it warmed my heart to see him hold our baby. He moved Layla's hat to show me her dark hair, much darker than that of our other children. I briefly recalled the dream I had before expecting her. I told her we waited a long time for her and thanked God for getting her to us safely.

After having babies, I typically stay at the hospital for three or four nights, but this time I stayed for two. Since it was not our normal hospital, it didn't feel as homey. I also missed my other kids terribly. I knew Brandon was stretched thin at home, even though he would not admit it. Plus, since our new home was larger, I thought it would be easier to get away in my room or somewhere in the house by myself with Layla to focus on healing and helping her adjust to the world.

I was wrong. Every time I nursed Layla, it seemed like all three of the little boys came over to my lap. If I tried to go to my room, they'd cry at the door. It was not the best circumstances, and I wished I had just stayed one day longer because that first day and night at home were rough. I sat on the couch in intense pain and wondered how I would ever feel better again. The first night, I tried to get out of bed to feed Layla, and I could not get up no matter how hard I tried. I did not have the bed railing to pull myself up like I did with the hospital bed. Brandon gave up his evening to lay next to me in bed at 8:00 PM in case Layla or I needed anything. As the week went on, I did start to feel better which was good because I needed to feel my best for what was about to come.

Like Landry's first days, our family had an illness shortly after Layla's birth. This time, it was the stomach flu. Almost all the kids had diarrhea and horrible stomach cramps. Layla was about two weeks old, and she came down with it. Brandon and I had just gotten the other little ones to bed, and we were changing Layla into her pajamas. Suddenly, she threw up. It was much more abundant and forceful than her usual spit up. We gave her a bath, and she promptly wanted to breastfeed again. I've read that you should breastfeed your baby on demand even when they have the stomach flu. So, I went ahead and fed her. She started throwing up again at the start of the feeding. I took her over to the kitchen sink and yelled for Brandon who was cleaning up the changing table from the first vomiting episode.

As Brandon was coming into the kitchen, Layla gave us quite a scare. Her limbs all tucked into her body, and she was limp, like a rag doll. Her lips were slightly blue, and she was unresponsive. I was yelling incoherently and frantically patting her back. I honestly thought my baby girl was dying right before our eyes. I realized how precious life is and how quickly it can all come to an end. Her life and my hopes for her future flashed before me. I begged God to help and let her be okay. This all seemed to go on forever, but it was probably under a minute. By the time Brandon had 911 on the line, Layla was conscious but not crying. She was wide-eyed and looking around very quietly, not making a sound. She looked like she was stunned by what had just happened. I handed her over to Brandon and went upstairs to change my clothes. Thankfully, she started to cry after I handed her over. Still concerned, I announced I was taking her to the hospital with or without the paramedics.

The paramedics arrived in about five minutes, but that also seemed much longer. The paramedics were thrilled to hear a screaming baby when they entered our home. After hearing what had happened, they promptly informed us that she "vagaled out" or had a vasovagal response from vomiting. This was reassuring to me. I related it to the breath-holding spells Lily had when she was about a year old. She would get mad and pass out. I recalled how she too, looked like a ragdoll when she did this. It was scary, but she would always come out of it after a few seconds.

The paramedics gave us options. They could take Layla to the hospital, but I would have to follow because of COVID-19, or I could take her myself. I did not want to take her myself because I would not be able to monitor her while driving. So, I followed the ambulance as they took my newborn baby to the hospital. They did not have their lights or sirens on and drove carefully with the precious cargo. They even drove under the speed limit at times.

By the time we got to the hospital, I started breaking down. I was worried it might happen again. I was afraid Layla would not be able to keep her feedings down and would require an IV. I pulled myself together, declaring I had to be strong for her, and got out of the car.

By the time I got to the registration desk, I started breaking down again as I told them I was there to see my newborn baby who was brought by ambulance. They promptly got me back to her room. The nurses and doctors had her undressed and were examining her as she screamed with objection. They got information from me, and I told the story about what had happened for the first of many times while at the hospital.

Minutes later, everyone had left the room. It was just me and Layla. They had told me I could feed her, and she seemed to want to eat, so reluctantly, that is what I did. As I was feeding her, I realized I packed everything she needed but neglected to bring a change of clothes for myself in case she got sick all over me again. Thankfully, she kept the feeding down.

Just as Layla and I were beginning to relax, we were informed that they were going to keep her overnight for observation. Then, a team of nurses came in to do an EKG, COVID-19 test and urinalysis. The worst was the urinalysis because it required catheterization. It was traumatizing for us both. I recalled the catheterization I had two weeks before and the trouble it caused giving me my very first UTI. I prayed it would not cause a UTI for Layla. I was moved when I heard one of the nurses ask another nurse if her shift was over. The nurse said, "Yes, but I will stay for her (Layla); it's only an hour."

I figured they probably don't get the opportunity to work with newborns very often which is a very good thing. Thankfully, all the tests were normal. After a couple of hours in the emergency room, a very kind nurse wheeled Layla and me to our room on the children's floor. By this time, Layla was so exhausted that she didn't wake up as we moved her to her bed. She looked so sweet but slightly miserable. She had this red mark on her eye from birth that darkened after being upset. It was bright red by this point. I snapped a quick picture of her as she slept and sent it to Brandon. He was heartbroken to see our two-week-old in the hospital, but we were so relieved that she was okay and in good hands.

We spent two days in that room. Layla slept most of the time and didn't have any vomiting episodes, nor did she pass out. I focused on feeding, changing, and holding her. I also used the chance to watch TV, which I rarely have time for at home. I enjoyed the peace and quiet but not without guilt about leaving Brandon to care for sick kids at home, yet again. I realized I rushed out of the hospital when Layla was born and missed out on time for quiet rest and healing, but God turned this situation around into an opportunity to make up for that time in a hospital that felt more like home. It was time for Layla and me to focus on bonding and healing.

When we got home, everyone was so excited to be together again. I found it interesting that Landry went directly to Layla instead of me. He squatted down to look at her and talk to her as she was sitting in her car seat. Just a week earlier, he told her to get her shoes and socks on and go "bye bye" because she wouldn't stop crying. I guess the time apart made him realize how much he loved her and wanted her to stay.

# Our Homeschool

I would like to start this chapter by saying homeschooling is something I have been called to do, but that isn't the case for everyone. I could spend hours doing lesson planning or looking at curriculum because God has put that passion in my heart. There are other moms who are just as passionate about planning classroom parties, volunteering at their children's school, or attending PTA meetings. Brandon and I do not disparage those who educate their children by means other than homeschooling. In fact, as we began to homeschool, it quickly became apparent to us that homeschooling is not common. Through the years, we have learned to embrace this. The experience helps prepare our kids for the many times in life when they will need to do what God asks them to do or not do even if that means being different.

*Do not conform any longer to the pattern of this world, but be transformed by the renewing of your mind. Then you will be able to test and approve what God's will is- his good, pleasing and perfect will. - Romans 12:2 NIV*

Long before I began homeschooling, there were experiences and life lessons that prepared me. In 2006, I started my career in child abuse prevention as an intact family caseworker. I worked with parents who still had their children. Sometimes, cases were not successful, and the children needed to be removed. One night, I had to find a home and place some children in foster care. I had observed this process before, but it was not something I had done. I had no idea what I was doing, but I tried to stay calm. Then, one tiny step popped into my head, and that led to another and then another. By the end of the night, those children were safe and sound in a foster home. I knew as I was going through that process that God was helping me and teaching me to take one small step at a time, and that will lead to another.

I use this life lesson with my kids daily. When I get overwhelmed, I remind myself to take one step at a time. When the kids have a tricky math problem or assignment and say, "I can't" or

"I don't know how to do it," I ask them to start with one small step they do know.

*We can make our plans, but the Lord determines our steps.*
*-Proverbs 16:9 NLT*

I hesitate to give a break-down of our day because the truth is, it is constantly changing. There are things that throw a wrench in our day often such as messes, boo boos, a cranky toddler, migraine, and the list goes on. Our homeschool is far from perfect and I want to preface that before I say anything more about it. There have been so many days that we do school on the living room floor as a toddler plays next to me or sits in my lap because they refuse to have it any other way.

I have read a lot of books and seen documentaries about other homeschool families and I often end up feeling like I don't measure up. That is the last thing I want my readers to feel. Every family is different and so is every homeschool. If you're reading this as a homeschool mom and your children are loved, have their basic needs met and are progressing academically, you're doing a great job! Kids have this amazing way of learning when they are ready and when you least expect it. Please keep all this in mind as you read about our homeschool day.

Every morning, I strive to get showered, dressed, and make the bed before starting my day with the kids. I find I am much happier, patient, and productive when I am out of my pajamas. At 7:00 AM, Lucian, Leland and Landry get up and I get them settled with breakfast and a cartoon like *Curious George*. Then, I do some bible study nearby in our homeschool room before Layla wakes up. Bible time is very important to me. It fills me up and sustains me through the chaos. Things just seem to run a lot smoother, and I am much happier after I get my bible time in. If I miss a day, I certainly feel it and the kids probably do too because I get irritable. My daily bible-reading goal is to read one chapter each of the Old Testament, New Testament, Psalms and Proverbs. I don't always get it all done but do my best. I'm starting to realize that the most important thing isn't how much I read but that I fully understand and remember what I read.

*Jesus answered, "Everyone who drinks this water will be thirsty again, but whoever drinks the water I give him will never thirst. Indeed, the water I give him will become in him a spring of water welling up to eternal life." - John 4:13-14 NIV*

After my morning bible time, Layla wakes up and I get her and Landry dressed. Lucian and Leland pick out their clothes and get dressed independently. Some families homeschool in their pajamas which is perfectly fine. Having everyone dressed for the day is just my personal preference. We like to break up routine and get out a couple of mornings a week. We usually go to a park, library, or a store. It is nice for all of us to be dressed and ready to go.

Once everyone is out of their pajamas, Layla and I have breakfast. By that time, the boys already had breakfast but usually eat a bit more with us. Then, I clean up and do a load of dishes and/or laundry. Having a tidy home is important to both Brandon and me, so I try to pick things up as we go. If I don't, messes get out of hand in a hurry.

Logan and Lily are up and dressed around 8:00 AM. After they have eaten breakfast, I have them watch over the littles while I do workbooks with Leland and Lucian. Lucian requires one-on-one attention, but he also benefits from observing Leland. Leland loves school, so he sets a good example. Additionally, Lucian is competitive, so he makes sure he stays ahead of Leland when it comes to academics.

As you may recall, one thing I was surprised to learn before I started homeschooling was it does not take six hours a day which is what I expected. My young children only do about thirty minutes of bookwork a day. If I push them to do more than that, they start to hate doing it. As they get older, we will slowly increase the time. Thirty minutes may not seem like much, but our school day goes beyond the bookwork. I sneak in a lot more learning throughout the day. We play with magnetic letters and games that help with reading. We read books, sing songs, and talk about social studies topics like community helpers or science themes like weather and seasons. I love to go for walks and watch how God pops learning opportunities right in front of us such as plants, insects, colors, shapes, and letters.

The younger boys absolutely love early elementary computer programs. I let them use these sparingly. I've found that they learn on these programs initially but eventually just want to play the games.

A day or two a week, we like to pile up blankets and do bible study. It can be a challenge because of the age gap, so we do a variety of things. We usually read bible stories for the younger children. Logan, Lily and I are going through a book that references scripture, asks questions and has various topics to discuss. On weekends, Brandon and I use a family devotional book. It is more hands-on and includes pre-planned activities.

We like other group learning activities too like science experiments, art projects or cooking. The kids love constructing volcanoes. One time, I ordered owl pellets for Logan and Lily to dissect. They had a lot of fun with it.

The kids have a natural interest for learning. Lucian and Leland frequently draw at the kitchen counter, so I keep paper, crayons, markers, and colored pencils easily accessible. They love to copy words and pictures from cereal boxes.

Logan and Lily watch a lot of educational videos on topics that interest them. Lily likes cooking, cake decorating and crafts. Logan loves computers. So far, he has built two computers from scratch. He learned how to do this on his own with no guidance from me or Brandon.

The kids often learn when I least expect it. I worried about how I was going to teach Lucian to use scissors. Then, one year around Christmas time, we were visiting my parents, and Lucian spent almost an hour cutting out pictures from a Christmas toy catalog. We took his clippings home and laminated them. He loved it! A few weeks later, he was cutting words out and following along dotted lines with no problem.

We have had so many other spontaneous learning incidents that remind me God is helping us every day. One time, Leland, at the age of three, came to me with a fabric map of the United States, and we sat and studied it. I showed him which state we live in. He pointed to various states, and I identified them.

Another example, Lucian went through a phase where he always asked what time it was, which gave me the opportunity to help him identify the numbers on the clock and learn to tell time. Calendars are fun for the kids too. When we have something exciting coming up, we mark it on our calendar and cross off each day as we get closer to the event.

The littlest ones are learning too, probably more than I realize. It warms my heart to see Landry or Layla sitting in the middle of the floor looking at books. I like to have Montessori-type toys for them such as mixing bowls, manipulatives, and lacing toys. One week, I noticed Landry and Leland kept walking around the house with a set of old keys, trying to find a door lock that matched. So, I got them some play locks with keys, and they are a big hit. I strive to create a fun environment in our home that fosters a learning lifestyle that lasts a lifetime.

After our morning schoolwork, we usually go outside when the weather permits until it is time for lunch. I love the fresh air and the kids love to run around or ride bikes. It really burns off their excessive amounts of energy. As the kids play, Lily usually asks me what we are having for lunch that day and helps me decide what to make. Lily loves to cook and often makes our lunch herself or at least helps me quite a bit. This can be a hectic time for us. We are all getting hungry and tired by this point.

One thing I like to do when we are trying to make lunch is let the kids watch books being read on YouTube. Other times, they watch bible stories or video lessons to reiterate what our books are teaching. For example, the skeletal system or ancient civilizations. Audio books are great to listen to while we are eating lunch. I use the Audible app. It keeps the mood calm and quiet.

The older kids use an online curriculum that teaches via video. It includes all assessments and practice. It tracks progress and grades everything as they go. They typically have about an hour to work on their schoolwork in the morning. After lunch, they get back to their studies. I sit with them in our homeschool room at noon while Layla and Landry are napping, and Lucian and Leland are having quiet play time. During that time, I provide extra help with Math, English, or whatever they need. Brandon is the math expert, so sometimes, the older kids wait for him to get off work to help with math. Other times, I watch the videos and learn right along with them, so I can help them.

Around 1:45 PM, I start getting snack ready. I pour four cups of juice and put a couple of snack items out. Landry and Layla usually wake up around 2:00 PM which is when I start work. Logan and Lily watch over their younger siblings as they have snack and then play. They earn a weekly allowance for doing this, and they do well. It helps all the kids to be more independent.

Brandon is off work at 3:30 PM. At that time, Logan and Lily finish their schoolwork if they have anything left for the day. Then, they have some free time and get ready for their evening activities.

My dad is very helpful and chauffeurs the big kids to wherever they need to go in the evenings while I work. Lily goes to gymnastics and youth group. Logan goes to diving and Pokémon tournaments at a local card shop.

Once Brandon is settled after work, he often takes the kids outside to play. He also likes to take them for a drive to find trains. Leland and Landry love finding trains. Brandon seems to get just as excited as they do when they find one.

Around 5:00 PM, Brandon makes dinner. I try to time my meal break so I can have dinner with them and help clean up. After dinner, Brandon usually helps the boys take their showers while I take Layla for a quiet walk. I like to use that time to point things out for Layla and teach her new words like "doggie" and "flower." Then, I give Layla a quick bath before returning to work. When it isn't shower night, we all go for a walk together.

Once the kids are all in their pajamas, they watch about thirty minutes of TV. We try to stick to shows like *Super Why*, *Yo Gabba Gabba* or *Imagination Movers*. Then, it's time to brush their teeth and put them to bed. Brandon often does the bedtime snack, TV show and teeth brushing by himself while I am working. I can usually step away from work long enough to say bedtime prayer and give hugs before they go to bed.

My shift ends at 10:30 PM, and that is when I unwind with God. After reading a bit more in the Bible, I write a summary of highlights in my own words in my journal. A few times a week, I write to God about my worries and thank Him for the good things He has blessed me with and/or helped me with. I also ask for forgiveness for my latest sins. Then, I write a section I call, "Reflection." That is where I write whatever comes to mind. It is usually positive and encouraging and often comes out as scripture.

Well, there you have it, a day in the life of the Kruep family homeschool. Second to God's help, teamwork is key to our homeschool running smoothly. Brandon and I have always worked well as a team. Neither of us work harder than the other. We both give it our all every day. If there is a day that one of us is tired or doesn't feel well, the other picks up the slack without resentment because it doesn't happen very often. Most of all, we have God guiding us and giving us strength and wisdom to keep going.

Logan and Lily are a really big help too. As the younger children get older, they will learn more responsibilities. In the meantime, they are learning how to work together as a team through observation.

*I look up to the mountains- does my help come from there? My help comes from the Lord, who made heaven and earth!*
*-Psalm 121:1-2 NLT*

# Family of Eight

*Children are a gift from the Lord; they are a reward from him. Children born to a young man are like arrows in a warrior's hands. How joyful is the man whose quiver is full of them! He will not be put to shame when he confronts his accusers at the city gates. -Psalm 127:3-5 NLT*

Like homeschooling, having more than two or three kids is quite different from the norm today. We often get disapproving glances when we all go out in public together. We are frequently asked if we are done having children. On the contrary, there are times we meet older couples who commend us for having so many children, and report that they raised five or six kids of their own and now have multiple grandchildren. These couples always seem to be joyful and calm like they have just ran a marathon. They are fulfilled and happy to have rest.

Having a new baby never got old for me or Brandon. We doted over all of them as if each one was our first. We went above and beyond to make sure they were clean, happy, safe and healthy. We got excited about each milestone they reached. That didn't stop when the kids grew out of the baby stage. We celebrate all their accomplishments and take care of them to the best of our ability.

At times, I am humbled when I watch Brandon with the kids. God doesn't want us to have all these kids just because of my love for children, but because of Brandon's love for them too. While I like the quiet activities and teaching, Brandon makes them laugh and finds active games to play with them. At night, he watches our youngest ones on the baby monitors to make sure they look okay, and their rooms are at comfortable temperatures. He has gotten out of bed on cold nights to cover them up when they kicked their covers off. He has given them extra baths when their diaper leaked overnight. He almost always turns their tears into laughter. He is so kind and respectful to our older children. He talks to them like friends, yet they respect his authority.

Brandon also helps a great deal around the house. He loves to cook! He does our grocery shopping weekly. He prepares most of our evening meals. He is a tidy person, so he always seems to be picking up. On weekends, he does a few loads of laundry for me, himself and the four younger children. He sorts it all into laundry baskets and I put it away. Thankfully, Logan and Lily do their own laundry.

Someone once asked me what I would do if I had more spare time. I said I would probably work out more which is true, but I don't really require a lot of "spare time." Spending time with my kids is what I choose to do. I love to hear them laugh and see how excited they get when they learn something new. I love how I can sit on the floor and play with something like Legos, and one by one, they join me. I love snuggling up with a book, memorizing the moment with all my senses because I know it will not last long.

Logan and Lily have grown past snuggles and toys and our relationships have evolved over the years. I love to converse with them throughout our day. We bounce ideas off each other and talk about things we have recently heard, seen, or learned. We encourage each other. Sometimes, one of them tags along on my walks with Layla just to talk. Lily and I often do our nails or go shopping. Brandon and Logan play video games together and talk about their gaming. Brandon and I like to play card games and watch movies with them once the little ones are all in bed. Our time with Logan and Lily is running out. We cherish the time we have with them.

As much as we love spending time with our kids, Brandon and I do need some downtime and couple time. We accomplish this by having a consistent sleep schedule for the younger kids. We strive to have the four youngest children in bed by 7:30 PM. Lucian and Leland typically talk while lying in their beds until 8:00 PM or so, but they stay in their room by that point. We also enforce nap or quiet time from Noon to 2:00 PM daily. This schedule gives Brandon and I the downtime we need to keep our home happy and functional. The kids seem to appreciate it as well.

# Following God's Plan

*Take delight in the Lord, and he will give you your heart's desires.*
*-Psalm 37:4 NLT*

After reading up to this point, you may be thinking, "How do you know you are really following God's plan?"

God gives us the desires of our hearts. As we grow closer to God, our desires line up with his plan. If we want things that are not in His plan, He changes our hearts, so we no longer want or hope for them. Similarly, if he wants us to do something that we don't think we can do, or don't want to do, he changes our hearts and even abilities, so that our plans line up with his.

*For God is working in you, giving you the desire and the power to do what pleases him. -Philippians 2:13 NLT*

As an intuitive person, I have taken note of my feelings when I do things that God wants me to do as well as things he does not. When I follow God's lead, I feel happiness and peace. I get extra energy and notice certain abilities I didn't know I had. I gain a healthy passion for the task. I feel relaxed and focused. I have a clear mind. Circumstances such as capability, time and money seem to align. For example, I was able to have six c-sections due to the miraculous way my body healed. Most women cannot have more than two or three c-sections.

Conversely, I have a negative experience when I sin or don't do things that God encourages me to do. I have a nagging feeling or guilt. I become obsessed and can't think about anything else. I feel less satisfied with all things in my life and don't enjoy anything as much. I also feel less focused and not as energetic. I notice myself getting annoyed easily instead of loving others unconditionally.

*No discipline seems pleasant at the time, but painful. Later on,*
*however, it produces a harvest of righteousness and peace for those*
*who have been trained by it. -Hebrews 12:11 NIV*

*But the fruit of the Spirit is love, joy, peace, patience, kindness, goodness, faithfulness, gentleness and self-control. Against such things there is no law. -Galatians 5:22-23 NIV*

This is a chart to help determine if you are following God's plan for your life. In general, if you are feeling the fruit of the Spirit listed in the scripture above, you are likely following God's plan. If not, keep praying!

| His Plan | Not His Plan |
|---|---|
| Focused | Distracted |
| Certainty | Confusion |
| Peace | Nagging Feeling/Guilt |
| Joy | Unsatisfied |
| Energetic | Unmotivated |
| Circumstances Align | Things don't work out |
| Healthy Passion | Obsession |
| Love | Irritation |

# Brandon's Love

*Don't just pretend to love others. Really love them. Hate what is wrong. Hold tightly to what is good. Love each other with genuine affection, and take delight in honoring each other. -Romans 12:9 NLT*

When I was around thirteen years old, Annie's mom was driving us home from gymnastics when Annie asked her an interesting question. "Who do you love more? Me or Daddy?"

I thought for sure that her mom's response would be she loves Annie more. I was wrong. Her mom promptly said, "Daddy."

Annie and I both gasped. "Really? How could you love him more than your own child?"

Sounding confident with her response, Annie's mom explained that she loves her husband more than her kids because he will always be with her, but her kids would all grow up and have their own lives one day. I may not have realized it at the time, but Annie's mom had a lot of wisdom.

Brandon's love continues to amaze me. He makes me feel safe and secure and has such a forgiving heart. He'll put my comfort before his own. We keep an ottoman full of blankets in our living room. The kids often take the blankets to various rooms to build forts. It is not uncommon for us to be left with one blanket as we wind down at night. Brandon always lets me have the one blanket. I often joke with him that I require daily journaling, scripture reading, listening to pastors, and Christian music to be half as Christ-like as him.

One night, we were up at 4:00 AM with newborn Layla. It was a typical overnight feeding and diapering. I usually did this on my own to keep her sleeping or at least very sleepy. If she woke up too much, she'd be awake for two full hours. This time, Brandon insisted on helping me by changing her diaper.

As I was lying next to her finishing the feeding, I felt wetness all around us. The diaper had leaked out the side because the tab wasn't secured properly. She was soaked, requiring a change of clothes and a new swaddle blanket.

As Brandon changed our bedding, I sat in the rocking chair with a very restless baby. I silently blamed Brandon for the rough night and seethed with frustration. Then, God asked me to think about how Brandon would have reacted if the tables were turned. He would not blame me or get frustrated. He would laugh it off and do what he could to get the baby back to sleep.

At that moment, I was reminded of what I had learned 10 years ago; Brandon has near perfect love for me, the closest love to Jesus' love that I will ever have on Earth. There is no other person I'd rather be with on this crazy journey. Lord willing, one day, our kids will all be grown up with their own lives and it will be just me and him. Therefore, apart from God, I love him most!

# Acknowledgments

Brandon, my husband, thank you so much for supporting me in everything I do! You keep me going. You are always on my heart and mind no matter what I do. Knowing I have you in my life gives me strength and confidence. I love you more than words can say.

Logan, you are the one who made me a mom. My life changed for the best when you came to me. You have grown into an exceptional young man. You are always willing to help others in any way. Your computer skills really helped me out from fixing my laptop to formatting the book cover. I had fun working with you and couldn't have done it without you.

Lily, my first-born daughter. You opened my eyes to a new type of love and bond that I never knew existed. You are my favorite shopping/hang out buddy. You are growing into such a beautiful young lady. I know you are going to impact the world with your godly character. You have such a big heart. Thank you for taking my photo for the back cover!

Lucian, I am so happy to have you in my life. I love your hugs and your smiles. You have such a love for Jesus, and he loves you so much too! You are so in-tune to the feelings of others and want nothing more than happiness for everyone. Your little brothers want to be just like you!

Leland, being a middle child is not easy, but you are very good at it. You play on your own and entertain yourself so well, but you are not afraid to show it when you need more attention. You are quick to apologize after losing your temper. You're always giving me flowers and hearts. You even open doors for me and Lily. You are such a gentleman!

My sweet "Baby Landry". You're not a baby anymore. You have excellent speech for a 3-year-old and have so many funny things to say. Most recently, instead of saying "blue fruit roll-up," you say "blue frow-up." It makes us all laugh and you love the laughter!

Layla, we are so happy you joined our family! Your dad and brothers love you so much and will always be your protectors…watch out future pursuers! Your sister will be your best friend forever, and I will always be your biggest fan.

Mom and dad, thank you for my safe, happy childhood and for having me involved in church as I grew up. You are the most giving people I know. You give your time and always shower the kids with gifts. You've dropped everything for us time and time again, and that has not gone unnoticed. I could never thank you enough for your help and support.

My mother and father in-law. Thank you for welcoming me into your family from the day we met. You raised an exceptional man. From the beginning, I knew Brandon was different, and he made me a better person. I attribute much of this to him being raised in a good home.

To my readers, thank you so much for taking the time to read this book. I hope it has inspired you to grow in your relationship with the Lord and follow His plan for your life.

Email: hisplanmanyblessings@outlook.com.
Website: www.planfaith.com for devotionals.

CPSIA information can be obtained
at www.ICGtesting.com
Printed in the USA
BVHW031503111022
649159BV00013B/1051